Catholics, Jews, and the Prism of Conscience

Responses to James Carroll's

Constantine's Sword: The Church and the Jews, A History

edited by Daniel Terris and Sylvia Fuks Fried

The International Center for Ethics,
Justice and Public Life

The Bernard G. and Rhoda G. Sarnat
Center for the
Study of Anti-Jewishness

Brandeis University
Waltham, Massachusetts

ISBN 0-9620545-2-6

Office of Publications
©2001 Brandeis University
R150

Table of Contents

Preface

On January 22, 2001, Brandeis University hosted a special
symposium to coincide with the publication of a major
new book by James Carroll, *Constantine's Sword: The
Church and the Jews, A History* (Houghton Mifflin, 2001).
Carroll's book maps the 2,000-year course of the history
of the Roman Catholic Church's relationship to Judaism
from the time of Jesus to the Holocaust and discusses
the crisis of faith it has provoked in his own life as a
Catholic. James Carroll describes his book as "history
as refracted through personal conscience." His previous
work includes nine novels and a memoir *An American
Requiem*, which won the National Book Award in 1996.

The Brandeis symposium was divided into three sections:
"*Constantine's Sword*: The Historians' Perspective"
(moderated by Edward Kaplan), "Between Catholics and
Jews" (moderated by Krister Stendahl), and "History
as Refracted Conscience" (moderated by Daniel Terris).
Carroll was joined by a distinguished panel of scholars
who examined the troubled history of relations between
Catholics and Jews. The events also served as an
opportunity to explore some of the issues that face all
people who look deeply and critically at abuses of power
within their own tradition.

Introduction

Daniel Terris

Humankind has much to regret about the last quarter-century, but one development that has reached nearly every corner of the globe is heartening. Out of the 20th century's whirlwind of violence has emerged a series of creative and poignant efforts to confront the tragedies of the past. South Africa's Truth and Reconciliation Commission; dialogue groups across ethnic divisions in places like Bosnia and Northern Ireland; educational programs designed to encourage young people to face the consequences of the Holocaust and other catastrophes; formal apologies by political and religious leaders—these few examples merely hint at the wealth of responses to the deeply-felt urge to confront the past and the search for ways to limit its lingering traumas, as new generations move forward with their lives.

"Memory" and "reconciliation" have become watchwords of the contemporary condition. Sometimes, it may seem, they roll off the tongue too easily—we are in danger of losing the substance in the service of the rhetoric. Democrats and Republicans in the United States, for example, began to speak of "reconciliation" in the wake of a bitter contest over votes in Florida. The word, in that context, rang hollow to anyone who watched even a few minutes of the gripping testimony—before Archbishop Desmond Tutu's Truth and Reconciliation Commission—of mothers of black South Africans who wanted to know the truth about the fate of their children.

If we have learned anything from this new emphasis on the process of memory and reconciliation, it is that it matters a great deal how we go about it. As we look back at the acts of violence, persecution, and terror that have shaped so much of human history, the process exposes our deepest vulnerabilities: the grief, the fears, and the anger that run below the surface of even the most contented among us. So it does matter how we do it. Empty rhetoric, superficial attention, the rush to "put all this behind us"—the wounded heart cannot be fooled.

The recognition of the importance of memory and reconciliation has spread to an extraordinary extent to many corners of world. But the battle to encourage people to face the past in ways that are genuinely searching, healing, and capable of inspiring true change, is just beginning. The temptation to make "reconciliation" an automatic part of our political and moral rhetoric is strong. Whatever we profess in theory, in practice we all tend to avoid rigorous self-scrutiny and painful candor. But self-scrutiny and candor are fundamental to any effort at reconciliation that will convince those upon whom history has left its mark.

One focus of the essays in this collection, *Catholics, Jews and the Prism of Conscience*, is the 2,000-year history of the relations between Catholics and Jews. Our occasion is the publication of James Carroll's book, *Constantine's Sword: The Church and the Jews, A History*. Carroll traces what he calls a "narrative arc" stretching back 2,000 years. He argues that Christian hatred and exploitation of Jews have a shameful pride of place at the heart of the Roman Catholic tradition. The writers of this volume explore and debate his contentions about the specific features of Christian antisemitism.

In addition to exploring the *content* of James Carroll's work, these contributors have also paid attention to his *process*. *Constantine's Sword* is not only a book about Catholics and Jews; it is also a book about power, and specifically about the way that an institution, founded on glorious ideals, swelled with conviction of its own sense of rightness, could proceed with extraordinary blindness and even malice regarding the consequences of its behavior for those outside its fold. Roman Catholicism is far from alone in its failings. The blindness of other faiths, other nations, other races, even of individual institutions may sometimes be on a much smaller scale, but the patterns of power are unmistakable. So are the correctives: vigilance, self-examination, and the willingness to encourage and tolerate the most intensive scrutiny of principles, motivations, and actions.

The narrative arc that James Carroll traces begins in insecurity and ends in tragedy, following the Christian relationship to Judaism from the time of Jesus to the present. Carroll's story paints an unsparing portrait of Christian hatred and mistreatment of the Jews, but it is not a story of unmitigated evil. There are acts of overt cruelty committed by the representatives of the institutional Church itself, to be sure—the horrors of the Inquisition or the construction and reconstruction of the Roman ghetto.

More often the story is one of ambivalence, of competing ideals that eventually lead toward disastrous consequences for the unprotected. Carroll makes it clear that many Church theologians, like Augustine, argued valiantly, often against the current of their times, that Jews should be protected from slaughter. But the terms of Jewish preservation were also telling. Augustine wished to preserve the Jews as degraded witnesses to Christian triumph. Carroll argues that this line of reasoning merely postponed catastrophe, allowing anti-Jewish sentiment to flourish in the field while Church fathers could disavow its excesses.

The end point of Carroll's narrative arc is the Shoah and its enduring memory in both the Jewish and Christian imaginations. The erection of the giant cross at Auschwitz is the starting point for Carroll's reflections on competing understandings of death and martyrdom, and on the meaning of the cross itself as a symbol of Christian dominance.

In *Constantine's Sword*, James Carroll paints himself as a critic from within, a committed Catholic who sees antisemitism as pervasive but not fundamental. He vigorously challenges the notion of the inevitability of Christian antisemitism; his history points to many heroic figures in Catholic history who drew on alternative strands of thought to promote a more inclusive Church. But Carroll also challenges the idea that the tragedy can be laid at the feet of "the sons and daughters of the Church," rather than at the feet of the institution, "the Church as such." In *Constantine's Sword*, he models what he believes the Church itself needs to undertake—a self-conscious attempt to identify and disavow the ways that Roman Catholicism made antisemitism central not only its behavior but to its theology. Every page of the book rings with Carroll's conviction that the process of self-scrutiny has every prospect of success, that Christianity's own values, resources, and traditions can fuel it, and that Jews and Catholics have everything to gain from an enhanced relationship that squarely faces history.

One challenge for any reader of *Constantine's Sword* is to participate in the demanding process that James Carroll has modeled—looking at the history of Catholics and Jews, to be sure, but also considering the insidious ways through which bigotry insinuates itself into power. It is easier to dissect the sins of our oppressors. It is more difficult to detect our own acts of exclusion, especially when we are so adept at articulating the rhetoric of justice and equality.

Jews have much to learn from the ways that James Carroll has probed the depths of his own tradition. In the particular story he tells, the Jews have most frequently been victims. But beyond James Carroll's narrative lie the instances when Jews have acquired power—in ancient times as well as in our own time. In those instances, Jewish ideals of justice have not always ensured equality and dignity for the "others" in their midst. At Brandeis, a Jewish-sponsored, nonsectarian university, it is particularly important to debate and to discuss how James Carroll has undertaken the process of looking backward, to avoid the trap of smug self-satisfaction that *Constantine's Sword* somehow validates the Jewish "cause."

We should also recall that Catholics and Jews share to some extent a history as unwelcome minorities in this predominantly Protestant country. If a courageous examination of Catholic antisemitism stimulates thoughtless anti-Catholicism, it is a disservice to everyone.

The writers of this volume examine a particular history through the prism of conscience which each of them brings to the task. Equally important, they focus on the nature of the prism itself—the ways that conscience is shaped by history and the ways that we can refine this lens to improve our sight and insight.

The contributors include historians, theologians, activists, and writers. They are Catholic, Jewish, and Muslim, bringing to their readings of *Constantine's Sword* a wide variety of methods, approaches, and perspectives. They look forward as well as backward as they consider the future of Catholic-Jewish relations, as well as its history. They grapple with questions of power and conscience in the Jewish and Muslim worlds, as well as in Roman Catholicism.

In a chapter of *Constantine's Sword* called "Between Past and Future," James Carroll writes: "It is the act of memory, cultivated in the present, in which past and future meet. Memory—as opposed to a mere cataloging of bygone episodes and doctrines," he continues, "presumes a personal commitment, a sense of urgency, an implicit hope. Doing history as an act of personal and institutional memory, and not merely as the repetition of records or the reassertion of conventional interpretations, is thus an act of responsibility to the future." By bringing together thinkers and activists to debate and discuss the past, present, and future of the complex relationship between Catholics and Jews, we are playing our own small part in making a candid confrontation with history an integral feature of the human condition.

The Church and the Jews

James Carroll

Constantine's Sword is a long and complicated book. It tells a convoluted story that unfolds over 2,000 years. Dozens of figures move on and off the stage. Some are well-known, such as Augustine, Aquinas, Maimonides, and Torquemada; others are obscure, such as Helena, Nicolaus of Cusa, Joseph Döllinger, and Edith Stein. Instances of high drama (the Crusades, the Inquisition, the Dreyfus Affair) compete with simpler events (a love affair, a pope opening up Rome to Jewish refugees from Iberia) that nevertheless have far-reaching consequences. The Holocaust at the center of the story both requires a response and shows the necessity of silence.

This history unfolds with full awareness of the dangers of the so-called lachrymose tradition, full awareness of Jewish agency and not just victimhood, and full awareness of the crucial fact that at key points this story could have gone another way. That said, it is apparent, even from a glance at the table of contents of *Constantine's Sword*, that this is a history marked by a nearly unbroken chain of assaults, insults, and persecutions directed by Christians toward Jews and by the Church toward Judaism. That chain extends from the definition of Jews as the murderers of Christ in the New

Testament, to the Church's claim to be the new Israel replacing the old Israel, to Constantine's elimination of the principle of tolerance. It includes the outbreak of anti-Jewish violence in the Crusades and the medieval effort to bring about the conversion of Jews. It extends to the ultimate suspicion of those Jews who finally do convert, and to the expulsions and the formation of ghettos. It includes the Enlightenment suspicion of Jewish difference and the stereotypes of Jews as both revolutionaries and capitalists. It culminates in the Church's modern use of antisemitism as a way of reconnecting with alienated masses and the widespread indifference to the fate of Jews during the Final Solution— indifference which became complicity.

Most often these tragic instances are considered unrelated episodes with responsibility placed at the feet of the individuals who participated in them. Blame is ascribed to individual Christians, those whom the Vatican calls sinful members of the Church. The blame is never ascribed to the Church as such. But *Constantine's Sword* insists on seeing these instances not as unrelated threads—to use the prosecutor's image—but as threads in a rope, a long narrative arc which draws the episodes together into one drama so that we can see how individual human choices in one age led to dark consequences in another. Once the chain of causality is established—how the indictment of Jews as the deicide people in the second century led to the blood libel in the 12th century; how the blood purity regulations of the Inquisition in the 16th century led to racial antisemitism in the 20th century—then the moral question has moved from the behavior of individuals to a flaw in the very character of the community: its structures, theology, liturgy, and preaching. The moral reckoning has moved inevitably to the Church as such.

While not agreeing with this reading, Eugene Fisher has put this issue most concretely: It is not enough to condemn Christian mobs for pouring out of churches on Good Friday to enact pogroms, as happened all over Europe through the centuries. One must also question exactly what those mobs had heard in those churches to prompt such reaction. A long sequence of bishops and popes have rightly condemned mob violence, but without asking of themselves how their own preaching and teaching had prepared for it.

It is of ultimate importance to me as a practicing Catholic that my Church has seriously undertaken the project of moral reckoning with this tragic past, beginning, especially, with the papacy of Pope John XXIII and more recently with the powerful personal witness of John Paul II. The current pope has done more to heal the breach between Christians and Jews, and in particular between Catholics and Jews, than any previous pope. The work I have done precisely as a Catholic is in response to the millennial call I heard from him. I have done this work drawing on and in concert with fellow Catholics, three of whom are contributors to *Catholics, Jews, and the Prism of Conscience*.

The culmination of John Paul II's witness was his historic act of repentance in 2000, coupled with his visit to Jerusalem and his reverencing of the Western Wall. This act symbolically reversed 2,000 years of Christian denigration of the Temple and Christian rejection of the rights of Jews to be at home in Jerusalem and Israel.

Momentous as these acts were, however, it is necessary to see them as the beginning of something, not the end. This historic act of repentance is reflected in two Vatican statements— "We Remember: A Reflection on the Shoah" of 1998, and "Memory and Reconciliation: The Church and the Faults of the Past" of 2000. That repentance was incomplete, in the first place, because it was abstract. The Pope apologized, yes, but without saying what exactly he was apologizing for. *Constantine's Sword* will tell you.

The Pope's historic act of repentance was incomplete, in the second place, because it omitted or even misrepresented key events in this history. In the Vatican's memory of the Final Solution, for example, "many"

Christians rescued Jews while "some others" participated in their destruction. In fact, as I once heard Eva Fleischner observe, the exact opposite is the case. *Some* Christians were rescuers, but *many* were complicit in the Holocaust. Not content to attribute the silence of Pius XII to difficult circumstances, "We Remember" turns the Pope into a hero of resistance on behalf of Jews, a dubious claim to say the least.

The historic act of repentance was incomplete, thirdly, because the acknowledged offenses were attributed far too narrowly as private acts and exceptions. The real horror of Christian antisemitism, so public and so constant, has yet to be fully confronted.

If the legacy of Jew-hatred and the violent persecution of Jews that culminated in the Holocaust is the result of individual moral failures on the part of Christians whose anti-Jewish attitudes were sinful, then the Church is right to insist that this history can be left behind by a new attitude of dialogue, expressions of civility, even acts of repentance for the sins of the Church's children. But if the virus of Jew-hatred that found its niche in the heart of Western civilization is the result of basic attitudes ingrained in Christian scripture, literature, and theology— Jews as the enemies of God—then much more is required of the Church than mere repentance. Furthermore, if through the centuries the Vatican has at times used its anti-Jewish policies as a way of advancing its own power, as suggested by the Roman ghetto or by the Church's association of Jews with revolution, then an authentic end of antisemitism requires also a re-examination of universalist absolutism. This absolutism—no true religion apart from the Church, no salvation apart from Jesus, no true orthodoxy apart from the authority of the pope—became a mark of the modern papacy and still characterizes many Roman Catholic pronouncements, most recently in September 2000 with the Vatican declaration *Dominus Iesus*.

For these reasons, *Constantine's Sword* ends with the call for a major reform of Christian structure and theology. It does so precisely because the sin of antisemitism is rooted not in the bad choices of sinful Christians, but in the behavior of saints: St. Ambrose, St. Louis, St. Thomas Aquinas, St. Francis of Assisi, blessed Pope Pius IX, whose contempt for Jews was regarded as holy because it in turn was rooted in the structure and the theology of the Church as such. Therefore, in order to end forever the sin of antisemitism and to assure, in Pope John Paul II's phrase, that no Holocaust can ever again take place, that same structure and theology must be questioned. That is why *Constantine's Sword* calls upon the Church first to fundamentally change the way it thinks of and teaches from its own foundational texts.

The gap between what Christian scholars assume about the anti-Judaism of the Christian scriptures and what lay people, even the well-educated, know is a scandal. All Christians must prepare to ask such basic questions as: Must the New Testament be set in tension with the Old Testament? Must the revelation of the Church be regarded as replacing the revelation of the Covenant? Must the Old Testament be regarded as prophecy, the New Testament as fulfillment? Certain fundamental structures of the Christian mind inevitably denigrate the religion of Israel: not only the ancient religion of Israel, but rabbinic Judaism which has flourished through the centuries. The anti-Jewish elements in the Gospels—in particular "let His blood be upon us and upon our children"—must be preached against themselves. This rarely happens in Christian churches.

The anti-Jewish slanders of the Gospels, however much the result of accidents of post-Temple history, must nevertheless be confronted as a revelation that the first generations of the Church proved capable of betraying something essential in the message of Jesus. This failure alone is enough to undercut notions of infallibility and triumphalist superiority over other religions.

Secondly, *Constantine's Sword* argues that the Church must make basic adjustments in what it says and believes about Jesus Christ, testing everything against the foundational truth that he was born, lived, and died as a Jew. The Church must say and believe nothing about Jesus Christ that denigrates the people Israel to whom he was absolutely devoted. There is no God of love and mercy, a Christian God, who has precedence over an older God of law and vengeance, a Jewish God. Eugene Fisher remarks that Jesus's Jewishness is well known by now to Catholics, and that is partly true, but even "Memory and Reconciliation," the Vatican document of the year 2000, lifts up Jesus's commandment of love as a new commandment, something that sets Jesus apart from Judaism. Jesus was never more Jewish than when he preached the God of love. The God of Jesus is the God of Israel, pure and simple. A Christian theology with that truth in its center must be very different from what is taught and preached in the Church today.

Thirdly, because the tradition of Christian hatred of Jews is intimately tied up with the Christian embrace of power that began with Constantine and continued with monarchical supremacist papacy, *Constantine's Sword* argues that the Church must confront this most basic question about itself. In taking on the trappings, structure, and ideology of the Roman imperium, did the Church betray its master who after all was murdered by that same imperium?

I know the objections to such questions and assertions. Is this the case of a liberal Catholic who is only yoking his reform agenda for the Church to the Holocaust? If so, is he not guilty of the worst blasphemy of all? It is a serious charge. It assumes the uniqueness of the Holocaust as an outbreak of evil that stands alone, and that is why the Vatican itself has emphasized the neo–pagan character of Nazi antisemitism and declared that its sources lie entirely outside of Christianity. It is certainly true that the particular evil of Nazi Jew-hatred and the individual character of the perpetrators of the Final Solution must always be insisted upon. The Final Solution was not the product, in Hannah Arendt's phrase, of an eternal antisemitism.

It must be said that Nazi evil did not spring whole from the Teutonic forest. What went before that evil in history prepared for it: not only Martin Luther's definition of the Jew as the negative "other" of the German *volk*, but also the Inquisition's definition of the *converso* as the enemy within, the blood-sucking parasite so attached to the body of Christendom as to require its violent removal. Beyond the particulars of Germany, what went before that evil in history prepared a whole civilization to be indifferent when it showed itself as evil aimed especially at Jews.

Constantine's Sword is a narrative history with a beginning, a middle, and an end, which is Aristotle's formulation. Every drama, he says, has conflict, crisis, and resolution. The crisis is the turning point, the moment of reversal and the epiphany. At the epiphany, the hidden action of the narrative is revealed. Aristotle's word for that moment is "catastrophe," which is a chilling word in our context, since the Hebrew translation of "catastrophe" is *shoah*.

The Holocaust, however unique, is also a revelation, an epiphany of a deep-seated evil that has infected an entire civilization, which is why the history of the Holocaust should not be considered in Jewish Studies—as it is in almost all academic institutions—but in the core curriculum of Western civilization. The Holocaust in Jewish Studies keeps it a Jewish problem while the problem belongs to the whole culture. This is why 60 years after the event, key institutions of that culture—banks, museums, relief agencies, manufacturers, newspapers, the U.S. State Department, libraries, the library at Brandeis—are just beginning to confront their unfinished moral business with "the catastrophe."

And so what of the Church? If the government of Argentina can explicitly repent for sheltering Nazi war criminals as it did last year, why can the Vatican not explicitly acknowledge its role in helping some of those same Nazis flee to Argentina? Here again our gaze must go from the thread to the rope. The obsessive contention over the particular responsibility of Pope Pius XII during the years of the Final Solution is perhaps misplaced in this broader context. Robert Wistrich has suggested that an over-emphasis on papal absolutism as the key to the problem slights the sad history of the acquiescence of the German episcopacy. But what licensed that acquiescence, prompted it even, if not the concordat between the German Reich and the Holy See signed on July 20, 1933, an act not of Pius XII, but of Cardinal Pacelli.

We have to do more than continually protect the broad claims of the Vatican in this regard. Whatever one makes of the dispute about Pius XII—and that dispute is not resolved and one can presume it will not be for some time—it is quite clear that the silence of Pius XII is not the crime but the indictment. It is the indictment and the evidence. In literary terms, it is the epiphany and the revelation. Thus, the Church has a far more grave moral reckoning to do than its current account of Vatican policies during World War II. Catholic defensiveness in favor of Pius XII, including the still lively possibility of his beatification, suggests how very far the Vatican is from leading the way, or even following others, into this deeper reckoning.

The Vatican, however, is not the same as the Catholic Church. I assert this as a Catholic determined to be responsible for my Church. I accuse the Church of nothing of which I do not myself stand accused. Obviously, there are those who object that the changes I call for are changes that would simply mean the Church is no longer the Church. That objection, however, is rooted in an ahistorical notion of what the Church is and what it has been. In fact, if every reform I propose in structure and theology were implemented right away, the change in this institution would still be less drastic than the change it went through overnight when in the fourth century Constantine made the Roman Empire and the Christian Church the same thing. These changes would be less drastic, for that matter, than the change that the small community of Jesus's first followers underwent in the first century when their beloved Temple was destroyed by the Romans. They would be less drastic than the change that occurred in the Church in the 13th century when Aristotle was adapted by Thomas Aquinas and others as the new form of Catholic substance. The history of this Church, in other words, is a history of change. As this record suggests, the change is not always necessarily for the better, but the point is: to change substantially in response to the forces of history is a profoundly Catholic phenomenon.

Who am I to say so?

I say none of this on my own authority. The observation
has been made that much of what I argue is not new. That
objection does not undercut my argument; it *establishes*
it. I am a Catholic speaking out of the Catholic tradition.

The idea that Christian theology must be recast to
affirm the full and continuing validity and authenticity of
Jewish religion is not my idea. It is St. Paul's.

The idea that Jesus must be seen not as the sacrifice
offered to a violent God who took his life as a kind of debt
payment, but as a revelation that God already belongs in
love to everybody, is not my idea. It is Abelard's.

The idea that religious pluralism is a part of God's plan
and not a signal of corrupt relativism, as the present
Vatican sees it, is not my idea. It is Nicolaus of Cusa's.

The idea that the Church's attachment to power
has compromised its integrity, has at times made it
dangerous, especially to Jews, is not my idea. It is Joseph
Döllinger's and Lord Acton's.

I invoke not only popes and bishops who defended Jews,
and there were many. I invoke not only the beloved John
XXIII who inspired me, but who was himself first inspired

by the Jewish historian Jules Isaac. I invoke not only
the great figures of the reform-minded Second Vatican
Council—Karl Rahner, Hans Küng, and Bernard Häring—
and the Jewish theologian Abraham Heschel who inspired
them. I invoke this whole complex history itself. I invoke
all Catholics and Christians who have grappled with
these questions, finding themselves unable to follow the
self-exonerating and defensive lines of argument that
have issued and still issue from Rome. We are the Church
too.

Constantine's Sword begins at Auschwitz at that 23-foot-
high cross that was planted in the field abutting the wall
during the tragic dispute over the Carmelite Convent.
This cross became a symbol of pride for nationalist Polish
Catholics, while being a kind of sacrilege for many Jews.

From my earliest memories as a Catholic, I have loved
the cross. A cross has always sat on my writing desk
and it still does. But at the wall of the death camp, the
cross appeared to me in ways it never had before. The
cross at Auschwitz made the question of supersessionism
sharper than ever. Is the overwhelmingly Jewish character
of that graveyard of one-million-and-a-half Jews now to
yield before Christian claims?

This is not, as some would have it, an insignificant,
unseemly argument over victimhood. When Pope John

Paul II referred to Auschwitz as the Golgotha of the modern world, there were reasons to wonder what exactly was being said. After all, if Jesus had died at Auschwitz, he would have died there not as the savior of the world or as the messiah or even as a Catholic. Jesus would have died at Auschwitz, an unknown man with a number on his arm. That is all.

The cross at Auschwitz is a revelation and a requirement. It is a requirement that, before too glibly invoking Golgotha, we Christians learn, in the words of the late Paul Van Buren, to speak of Auschwitz from the perspective of the cross by first learning to speak of the cross from the perspective of Auschwitz. When we do that, we see everything differently. That is why, finally, when *Constantine's Sword* takes up the question of repentance, it proposes a return to the cross at Auschwitz:

> Therefore, the Christian Church should come to Auschwitz and perform a simple penitential rite. This rite must be conducted in silence to compensate for the sinful silence of the Church, but more to push beyond all the words that have come too easily. Silence does not preclude expression. The acknowledgment of sin requires expression, but the proper word of acknowledgment here is an act, a sacrament of the Church accusing itself.

The penitential rite would consist of a dismantling of this cross, a removal of the horizontal beam and uprooting of the vertical, a reversal of the instruction Constantine gave his soldiers. In this way, the cross would be returned to Jesus and returned to its place as the cause of his death, not the purpose of his life. For Jesus, the cross could have been nothing of conquest or power. For Jesus the cross could not conceivably have become a symbol of triumphalism nor a sign of the defamation of his own people.

To remove this cross is to begin the reversal of all that we Christians here confess. To remove this cross is to retrieve the cross as sign that God has come to a failed and sinful Church. Only by confessing itself as such can the Church fulfill its mission as witness to God's unconditional love for all. More important, to remove the cross from Auschwitz deliberately, reverently, and in the presence of living Jews would restore Auschwitz to those who were murdered here, asking nothing of them in return.

Toward a Universalist Mode of Discourse

Arthur Green

James Carroll's *Constantine's Sword* is a history of
Christian and specifically Roman Catholic attitudes
toward and treatment of Jews and Judaism over the
course of nineteen centuries. Beginning with an extended
meditation on the cross planted outside the Auschwitz
barracks and the controversy that continues to surround
it, Carroll unflinchingly traces the history of Christian
anti-Judaism all the way back to the Gospels themselves.
Over the course of more than 600 pages of narrative,
he takes the reader through the history of the Western
world—touching on politics, philosophy, theology, and
a host of other topics—all from the viewpoint of the
Church's "Jewish Question."

But this book is also James Carroll's own story, and
the weaving together of historical and personal narrative
is masterfully done. A former Paulist priest and still
a committed Catholic, Carroll gives an account of his
own adolescent spiritual strivings. His mother was the
dominant Catholic influence in his early life and the
way in which spiritual quest is nurtured by a search
for maternal love is a *leitmotif* that Carroll expresses

in touching and personally revealing ways. His later questioning of his Catholic faith and his struggles with the institutional Church are also part of the story.

In the concluding chapters, Carroll calls for the convening of a Third Vatican Council to complete the work of reconciliation that was so admirably begun by Vatican II under the leadership of Pope John XXIII. Carroll gives the present pope good grades for his devotion to continuing that work, culminating in his visit to Israel and his praying at the Western Wall in 2000. But he also decries the undercutting of Vatican II's intentions by the conservative forces represented in this same papacy. Special condemnation is placed on the ongoing papal resistance to democratization and the re-introduction of exclusivist claims to salvation, particularly in the recent encyclical *Dominus Iesus*. That document, issued by the Vatican in September 2000, stands in direct contradiction to the spirit of all that has been accomplished over decades of what seemed like real progress in interfaith dialogue, reaching beyond calls for "tolerance" to a real mutuality of respect and understanding.

I have tremendous respect for the daring moral courage and intellectual honesty of this book. I am also deeply moved by the personal character of Carroll's undertaking. It is always interesting to see in another person's story close parallels to my own religious journey, despite our great differences. We grew up and engaged in our seeking in the contexts of very different, and in those days really opposing, religious traditions. It has been the case for me over the course of 40 years that, although I live wholly within Judaism, as a seeker, a scholar, and a theologian—and I like to think I learn from exposure to all the world's great traditions—the significant other for me has always been Roman Catholic. My own faith and questioning over the years have been nurtured both by reading and by personal contacts with individuals raised within, and usually struggling with, the Catholic Church and their Catholic Christian faith.

Let me begin with the struggle. If we Jews are the original dissenters of the Western world, as Carroll suggests early in the volume, I heartily welcome him to the club. To stand up in sharp criticism of an institution and tradition you love is no easy matter. We in the Jewish community are new at that for different reasons than he is. Our historical role was as dissenters from truths the Catholic Church would have liked to believe were held universally. That is, we dissented from somebody else's religion, and we paid the price for it. But over the past quarter century, some of us have learned how vital it is to speak up clearly against actions and attitudes found among your own people and committed in the name of your own religion or in the name of an institution (a state, for example) that is in some way the embodiment of it.

Without minimalizing the complexities of the Middle East conflict, many words have been said and deeds done that diminish the good name of Israel, which is also the name of the entire Jewish people. Learning to dissent in the context of love and ongoing commitment, while well-meaning loyalists hurl accusations of perfidy and betrayal, is not easy. Knowing the moral anguish caused by such experiences vastly increases my respect for Carroll's undertaking.

So here it is, the history we have known to be true all along, laid out for all to see by a Catholic writer. This is something of vindication, to be sure, but it is all too sad and ugly to lead to any sense of triumph. The direct line that runs from the Gospel of John to the Crusades, through the ritual murder and charges of the desecration of the host, the Chmielnicki massacres (in which, incidentally, Jews and Catholics were fellow victims of Cossack Orthodox rage), the ghettos, the expulsions, the early and later pogroms of Eastern Europe, and into the Holocaust—that line has been clear to Jews all along. The viciousness with which this legacy of hatred was pursued through the ages—long after *ecclesia* was clearly triumphant over *synagoga* by any standard of measurement—looks like sibling insecurity. It is much like the story of the younger brother, never secure enough in his victory to stop beating his weakened older brother on the head, a clear token that he will never quite *believe* that he has been chosen to replace the firstborn. It is as though the key theme of Genesis—the endless anxiety of that younger brother, who we once were with regard to the older inhabitants of Canaan, the tale of Jacob and Esau, of Ephraim and Manasseh—has been placed on its head and turned against us.

Yes, the Church must fully admit its responsibility. In theological language, that means confessing its sin. It is the Church, the body of Christendom with all its attraction to worldly power that carried it to greatness, that needs to attest to its sin. The responsibility lies not just in the errant ways of some Christians who "distorted" or "failed to understand" the Church's message of love. Nobody in the world understands the game of casuistry better than the two of us, Jews and Catholics, and we will have none of it. I affirm and rejoice in the fact that Carroll allows for no evasion of real accountability by means of elegantly drawn distinctions.

So I am an enthusiastic supporter of James Carroll's call for a Vatican III. Too bad it is no more in his hands than in mine. But I want to push the agenda a bit beyond his own bold steps. We need to move toward a deeper psychological understanding of this sibling story as a whole, and especially its denouement in the Holocaust, an approach first suggested by Richard Rubenstein more than 30 years ago. Carroll does not sufficiently come to

31

terms, it seems to me, with the degree of anti-Christian rebellion that Nazism marks. In this sense, he leaves too much room for the Christian apologetic that points out the resurgence of Teutonic paganism and Wagnerian mythos at the heart of Nazism, and will thus attempt to absolve Christianity of responsibility for an ideology that is anti-Christian at its core. For this reason I believe that a true day or reckoning and repentance for the Church must deal with the deep ambivalence with which the peoples of the Roman Empire, and especially the fierce tribes of Northern Europe, accepted their submission to the rule of Christ.

The codes of violence, vengeance, and honor by which they had lived from time immemorial were vitiated when they were conquered in the name of this skinny Jew hanging from a tree. Yes, they accepted his love, longing for salvation from death and the promise of life everlasting. But they also must have resented him terribly for imposing on them a demand for love of neighbor, for contrition of heart, for doing good unto others, and, worst of all, for loving and forgiving their enemies. What manly Goth, Viking, Slav, or Roman ever lived that way?

So the love of Christ became Christian devotion, the Church after Constantine. The hatred of Christ was displaced and turned against the Jews, those who had foisted this 98-pound weakling of a savior upon them. Vengeance has been wreaked upon the Jews ever since. And some of it touches close even to the most sacred act of Catholic piety. Those who aspired to salvation through the Christian Paschal rite, the ritual ingestion of what the Church averred to be the very body and blood of God's martyred son, turned around and said of the Jews, their shadow people, the "bad" twin brother: They celebrate their Passover by consuming the blood of our innocent martyred Christian children. There are psychological factors here that one would have to work hard to overlook.

I am suggesting that true reconciliation between Jews and Catholics will not happen without examining and accepting the deep psychopathology of the Jewish–Christian relationship. Nazism was a horrible attempt by forces at the heart of Europe to break loose, to free it once and for all, of the yoke that links our two traditions and histories to one another. The distorted Nietzschean proclamation of freedom from the Christian ethos went hand in hand with the freedom to exterminate the Jews, the people who had, through Jesus of Nazareth, given that ethos to the world. If our recovery from the Nazi debacle is truly going to change us, all of that must be examined.

Of course it takes two to have a psychopathological relationship. We Jews for too long reveled in the moral righteousness granted us by our victimhood. Any hint of talk about Jewish complicity in the nightmare of our history, any sense that Christian exclusivism, for example, had been inherited from our claims of unique chosenness as God's only people, was dismissed as a cruel way of "blaming the victim." But our collective re-entry into the world of power politics and our often powerful voice as citizens in democratic countries no longer allows us the luxury of this dismissal. As we ask that Christians go farther than is comfortable in examining their history and attitudes in relation to us, we have some serious questions to ask of ourselves as well. The limiting of noble biblical ethical proclamations to one's fellow-Jew rather than extending them to all humanity, as found in many rabbinic commentaries, is unacceptable. The relative tolerance of halakhic authorities in the past for taking economic advantage of non-Jews, including governments, has to be re-examined and repudiated. The daily blessing that thanks God "for not having made me a gentile" is as worthy of rejection as the one in which we men are to thank God "for not having made me a woman," all apologetics not withstanding. The rabbis' demonization of Esau, the supposed ancestor of Christendom, and of Balaam, the prophet of the non-Jews, speak ill of our tradition.

For 2,000 years, we Jews were without worldly power, especially on the political stage. Yes, the Catholic Church has at times been drunk with power, and the call for Vatican III to step back from that place is appropriate. We, who are new to power and insecure about how much we really have, should learn the lesson well. Carroll's call for the Church to embrace democracy in an unambiguous way is also an important one. Here we Jews would seem to be in much better shape. Acceptance of democracy and its values scores high on any survey of Jews, especially in North America. But what is the relationship between our Judaism and the widespread identification Jews feel with democracy? We Jews justly take collective pride in the memory of Jewish individuals who contributed to the cause of civil rights in this country as well as in South Africa, even though most of these were quite alienated from Judaism and (especially in South Africa) some were Jewish communists. We should take less pride in Israel's one-time close association with apartheid South Africa as an ally and arms customer. We should take less pride in the past fear of most Jewish leaders to speak out against the Vietnam War because vocal Jewish protest might lead to antisemitism, or to speak out today against violations of human rights in the occupied territories, lest we be seen as divided in our support for Israel. In Israel the relationship between Jewish values and those of democracy is being put to a much more serious test and the results so far are not entirely encouraging.

It was Mordecai Kaplan who first spoke of the need for a Judaism that would truly take democracy seriously. As the Catholic must ask what democratic restructuring would leave of a hierarchy and how the Church could function without it, we must examine *halakhah*, the normative way of Jewish practice and ask how the introduction of democracy would change the most elementary structures of Jewish law. What will replace the old talmudic "order of women," for example, containing all the laws of marriage, divorce, and personal status, once women are fully integrated into a new legislative process? Oh, for a Yavneh II, if only we could!

With regard to exclusivity of claim, I strongly believe that our repentance has to take place together. This is *not*, I should emphasize, because the situation requires mutuality in change, nor does Carroll call for it in any way. To do so would be inappropriate. The sins of Christendom against the Jewish people are what they are, and it is the churches, all of them, that need to repent. I am not claiming that we share the blame for antisemitism over the ages. It is only the depth of Carroll's longing for change that calls forth in me a response that says: "Yes, and we, too, will have to change." Indeed, we need the Church to repudiate the exclusivity of its claim as a means to salvation. Our world has gotten too small and we are both too aware of other religions, including those that have their roots outside the biblical tradition, to speak the language of exclusiveness.

But we Jews also need to go back to the midrashic readings of Sinai, cutting through our own exclusivist language, exposing to the light of critical reappraisal, even the text that says the mountain is called Sinai because that sounds like the word *sin'ah*, hatred. This refers to the hatred God presumably feels (or perhaps that which we are to feel) for the "nations of the world" who did not accept God's Torah. We will also have to examine with conscience the biblical teaching on "chosenness" itself, asking whether re-interpretation of this concept in a non-triumphalist and non-exclusivist way is possible—or whether Kaplan was right in demanding that it be excised entirely from our liturgy. Dare we ask others to change and ourselves continue to speak, as we do in the weekly *Havdalah* service at the conclusion of the Sabbath, of a God who distinguishes "light from darkness, the holy from the profane, Israel from the nations"? When we ask ourselves the really hard question of the Holocaust— "Had we not been the victims, how many of us would have risked our lives and our children's lives to save gypsies, or gays, or Catholics, for that matter?"—we do not have the nerve to even try to answer. The next question—"Would our Judaism have demanded of us that we do so?"—is also one that we cannot ignore.

In turning so much of Carroll's Vatican III call back on the Jews, I by no means want to diminish my hope that his call be heard within the Church. It is also at moments like this when we Jews tend ever so briefly to envy Catholics for the centralization of authority that characterizes their tradition. They do change slowly, encountering lots of conservative resistance along the way, but, at least on the surface level of praxis and official statement, they change entirely. If any group of rabbis were to undertake the proposals I have made here, they would immediately be denounced by ten other groups of rabbis. If we could convince the Conservatives to join with the Reform in such a gathering, the Orthodox would use it as an occasion to pronounce their exclusive loyalty to authentic Judaism. Were the Modern Orthodox to join—and that is entirely out of the question—others would leap up to say how those traitors were never really Orthodox in the first place. Yes, we live happily without fears of a vindictive hierarchy or threats of excommunication. But some of us experienced a strong sense of *aggiornamento*, envy, after Vatican II. Let me say clearly that the great and positive changes that have taken place in the Catholic Church since the days of John XXIII and by those following in his noble footsteps, have made a real difference in the world. They have impressed us tremendously and challenged us.

But now let me come to the heart of the matter. We *need* each other. Catholics and Jews represent two great spiritual traditions of the Western world, nourished by the shared font of a common Scripture. We both hear and seek to fulfill the biblical call to be "a kingdom of priests and a holy nation." There is much that we still have to say to the world. The most essential teaching of Hebrew Scripture, that every human being is created in the image of God, has still not been heard. We share that Scripture, meaning the call of God to teach it to the world, even if we disagree sharply on some of the details of its demand on us (birth control and abortion, to name the big ones).

We live in a society gone mad in the pursuit of money to buy creature comforts undreamed of by prior generations and a hunger for ever more exotic experiences that seems to know no end. The gap between rich and poor grows daily, a situation not likely to be ameliorated by the new crowd in Washington. Millions are degraded by hunger, by disease—I think especially of the ravages of AIDS—by addictions, by the need to enter prostitution, sweatshop slavery, or other forms of degrading work just to feed their children. Meanwhile, we keep working harder and harder, longer hours, more overtime, and with more wage earners per family, resulting in less quality time with our children, even with ourselves. We Jews and Catholics have such important things to say about all this: love for one another, human dignity, the importance of time out, rest, the Sabbath. We share a prophetic tradition that speaks of God's special love for the poor and downtrodden. We also have to help post-modern urbanized Westerners to get back in touch with an inner self who is too frightened to come forth in the busy, rough-and-tumble world where we live most of our lives. But our inner self needs to be addressed and nurtured. We live in an age of great spiritual hunger and we need to support one another and others in responding to that need. Only in that way will human behavior begin to change, leading us toward greater harmony with the natural world in which we live and which is itself so gravely threatened.

We are coming out of an age that thought it knew better than the collective wisdom of ancient religious traditions. In the early 20th century, many thinking people assumed that science would have all the answers. The progress of scientific knowledge would turn aside the darkness and the need for religion would recede. But the opposite has been the case. Western science, for all its great and real accomplishments, has not become a source of ultimate values. Living in the shadow of Auschwitz and the constant threat of potential nuclear disaster has led millions of people in the past half-century to quest for some deeper truth. Many of those have turned away from the legacy of the West altogether, finding Judaism and Christianity both to be vacuous and morally bankrupt. But we believe this is not the case. The Western spiritual traditions, if read with an open heart and a discerning eye, have much to say about the engaged spirituality that is so urgently needed in our day. As we have seen the focus of our ultimate anxiety shift from the nuclear worry to the threat of ecological disaster, it has become clear that we must turn to the wisdom of all the world's spiritual storehouses. These now have to become the common property of all humanity. The translation of their insights into a more universalist mode of discourse is an urgent priority. The real role of religion in this new century will be to help in effecting the great changes in attitude toward ourselves, our environment, and the precious resources required for the very survival of our planet. The rapacious overconsumption and anxious desire of each generation for more, ever more, that has characterized our way of living, especially that of Americans, is going to end soon. For it to end peacefully and by change of heart—that is our shared work as people of faith. It is time to bury all the old hatchets, and bury them finally and deeply, so that we can set about the task that lies before us.

Reexamining the Church: An Ongoing Process

Eugene Fisher

I was present in 1973 at the first national workshop in the United States on Catholic-Jewish relations. One of the things we talked about at that workshop was whether the issues that we were dealing with could ever become part of the mainstream discussion within the Catholic Church, and within Christianity more generally. In retrospect, I think these issues have indeed become part of the mainstream discussion and *Constantine's Sword* will help emphasize their urgency and the urgency of the need to repent. Repentance presumes a self-reckoning, a reckoning of the soul, *heshbon nefesh*, and this is very healthy.

I think there are some lacunae in James Carroll's book. It is difficult to squeeze two millennia even into 700 pages and get everything right. I am not going to discuss those lacunae specifically, although I will mention a few in passing. Instead, I will examine James Carroll's agenda items for a proposed Vatican III.

From my point of view, the agenda items most directly related to the Catholic relationship with the Jewish people are numbers one, three, and five: the call for a re-examination of the anti-Judaism of the New

Testament; the proposal for a new Christology; and a call for a reaffirmation of repentance for the sins of the Church. Items two and four—those that ask the Church to think about questions of "power" and "democracy"—are related to the internal ordering of the Church and its relations with the world at large. I am more or less neutral on two and four, so I will focus on one, three, and five.

I agree with the goals that James Carroll advocates. We do need to look again at the New Testament and how we proclaim it from the pulpit and in our classrooms. We need to take seriously the Jewishness of Jesus and the fact that Jesus did not just happen to be Jewish. I would argue that the universal repentance for Christian sins against Jews over the centuries called for by Pope John Paul II should become part of the annual cycle of Catholic liturgy.

My central point is that all three of these processes that James Carroll calls for in a new Vatican III have already been launched by Vatican II. We need to assess where we are, so that we do not reinvent the wheel even as it is already rolling, albeit more slowly than some people would like.

Carroll argues, for example, that Christians need to learn to read anti-Jewish texts as if they were themselves Jews. This literature already exists, written both by Jews (Samuel Sandmel comes to mind) and Christians (such as Krister Stendahl). What we need to do is integrate that way of reading more effectively into our textbooks and into our preaching. I think that this is happening.

Sister Rose Thering did a study of Catholic textbooks and how they present Jews and Judaism, especially when dealing with scripture, the primary lens through which Jews and Judaism are presented in Catholic teaching materials. Her study showed a very grim picture in the late 1950s, before Vatican II. Those 1950s textbooks were brought to the attention of the Second Vatican Council, especially to Cardinal Bea, a biblical scholar who drafted the fourth section of *Nostra Aetate* precisely in order to readjust the Church's understanding of its sacred texts. Similar work has been done by biblical scholars, such as Raymond Brown, Mary Boys, Philip Cunningham, and John Townsend.

Frankly, I do not think that *Constantine's Sword* sufficiently takes into account the reality of where we are in the process today. These issues have become more and more mainstreamed within Catholic biblical scholarship. When I updated Sister Rose Thering's textbook study of Catholic teaching materials in 1976, I found that they had been profoundly improved since before the Council. Philip Cunningham of Boston College updated my study in 1992 and found that the teaching of "contempt"—the idea that God punished the Jews for killing Jesus by destroying the Temple—can no longer be constructed from contemporary Catholic textbooks. It is simply not there anymore. Yes, there are many shreds of contempt remaining in paraphrases of the New Testament, but the major elements of the anti-Judaism of early Church teaching have been removed. That is a major step forward toward a renewed reinterpretation and understanding of the New Testament.

James Carroll and I would probably agree that, while we have made progress in the classroom, we need much more work in our liturgical materials. The lectionary, our method of choosing which passages to give on Sunday and which passages of the New Testament to pair with passages from the Hebrew scriptures, need radical revision. The lectionary on one Sunday, for example, includes Matthew XXIII, which includes a problematic treatment of the Pharisees. Why not choose Matthew XXIV instead, which does not have these same problems? Likewise, why start Easter Sunday morning with a reading from Acts which, unless clarified in the homily, leads people to assume collective Jewish guilt for the death of Jesus?

We also need to examine how we present the Passion Narrative on Passion Sunday and Good Friday. In Rome and in many other dioceses throughout the medieval period, the Jews were often told to stay in their ghettos on Good Friday. The bishops would position troops around the ghetto to make sure that Christians coming out of church did not vent their anger on the Jews around them. If it was traditional to protect Jews on Good Friday, why did none of these bishops think to examine what was going on inside the church?

The Passion Narrative needs to be properly understood so that it does not cause harm as it did in the past. I think the will is there, but there is more work to be done. I agree that a Vatican III might attract the attention of liturgical people in Rome, but the theological foundation and the mandate already exists in the Second Vatican Council statement *Nostra Aetate*. James Carroll's book might have examined more fully the 1974 Vatican "Guidelines for Implementing *Nostra Aetate*," as well as the 1985 Vatican "Notes on the Correct Way to Present Jews and Judaism in Preaching and Teaching in the Catholic Church."

There have been many such documents and bishops' conferences around the world. The statements of the United States Bishops' Conference have been among the best; these statements led the way toward implementing

Nostra Aetate, beginning with the 1967 "Guidelines for Catholic-Jewish Relations," drafted by my predecessor of blessed memory, Father Edward Flannery. Carroll's book, in my opinion, slights the great achievements of Father Flannery and his generation of pioneers, leaving the mistaken impression that not much has happened between Vatican II and Carroll's own book.

James Carroll's third agenda was a call for a new Christology. Again, I think there is good literature on this by scholars such as John Pawlikowski, Paul Van Buren, Clemens Thoma, Franz Mussner, and others. When I first began to give talks, I had to give a short explanation of the Jewishness of Jesus to Catholic audiences. This would often shake up my listeners. Bishop Sheil of Chicago gave a talk stressing the Jewishness of Jesus before Vatican II, and somebody yelled, "How can you say these things? Jesus wasn't a Jew; he was a Catholic. You're not a priest; you're a rabbi." Bishop Sheil replied, "Well, thank you very much. They called Jesus a rabbi too. I take that as a compliment."

By and large, however, Catholics are much more aware today than they were in the past of the Jewishness of Jesus. *Nostra Aetate* tells Catholics directly that Jesus, his mother, and the Apostles were Jews. This emphasis is reflected again in the textbook studies. James Carroll is right that this understanding should permeate the teachings of the Church, and it has.

Finally, I will take up the issue of "repentance," the fifth of James Carroll's Vatican III proposals. I think that we should not take "We Remember" out of context. "We Remember" is the 1998 Vatican statement which called on the Church to repent for the sins that Catholics committed against Jews, including those actions that contributed to the events of the Holocaust. That document should be read within a series of statements on repentance going back to Cardinal Cassidy's statement in Prague in 1990. Cardinal Cassidy's document precipitated in turn statements by the French, Italian, Swiss, Dutch, Polish, German, Hungarian, and American bishops. In a very profound series of statements, each group of bishops stated very specifically the experiences of the Catholic people in their own countries during the war and focused on the need for repentance.

"We Remember" followed this long series of documents. That statement, in turn, led to more reflection, more statements, including one by Cardinal Keeler for the American bishops. Then, in the year 2000, came Pope John Paul II's "Liturgy of Repentance." He enumerated seven categories of repentance, repenting for the Church's sins for an entire millennium. One of the seven is devoted entirely to the question of the sins against Jews. That is a very strong statement in itself. The Pope repented in the name of the whole Church. He asked God's forgiveness in all our names.

Then the Pope went to Jerusalem and to Yad Vashem. He met with his fellow townspeople who were Holocaust survivors and he prayed there in the name of the Church. He went to the Western Wall, and he put a petition into a crack in the Wall asking God's forgiveness. There are no codicils or qualifiers or nuances in that petition, which is now housed in the Israel Museum. It is meant to be read maximally, not minimally, not to be diced up into little pieces for what it does not say. It is meant to sum up all of the previous activity on the part of the Church.

John Paul II has been leading us through the Jubilee year in terms of repentance. The sum of his statements is stronger and more powerful than "We Remember" alone. By focusing on "We Remember" alone, James Carroll misses this larger context. The Pope has led Catholics through a whole learning process very consciously, mindful of what his symbolic gestures signify. Pope John Paul II should be understood fully for what he has attempted to do. This process is not the end of the story. It is the beginning.

Journey of Moral Reckoning

Robert Wistrich

One of the closing remarks in *Constantine's Sword* is taken from Friedrich Nietzsche: "The man who stares into the abyss may well discover that it stares back." James Carroll has made a long journey of moral reckoning into the heart of evil, into the dark center of Catholicism, and into his own most intimate beliefs. What he has found makes for a wrenching experience.

He has looked unflinchingly into the long and tragic record of Christendom's dealings with the Jewish people and has found this record painfully wanting, deeply inadequate, even horrifying in parts. He has asked—from within his faith, to which he remains committed all the same, in spite of all—how can the cross that stands as a powerful symbol throughout this book be seen a world-redeeming event after Auschwitz? And how can the Church continue to proclaim that there is only one way: the unicity and salvific universality of Jesus Christ and the Church? Whether the Church actually proclaims this today is another matter that deserves discussion, but certainly Carroll offers us a highly critical interpretation of that controversial Vatican document issued in September 2000, *Dominus Iesus*. James Carroll asks his questions in light of the history of the Church and the Jews, in light of the history of Catholic responsibility for Auschwitz. At the same time he carefully shades the meaning of the term "responsibility," as he evokes the history of Christian triumphalism and the structures of oppression that he finds within it.

The book is a powerful indictment of what Carroll calls the "Constantinian" strand of imperialism in the history of the Church. Carroll describes the shadow of Constantine's sword, which he sees as reinforced by the legacy of medieval papalism, by the dogmas of the Counter-Reformation, and eventually by the choices made by the anti-modernist tendencies in the Roman Catholic Church in the 19th and 20th centuries. This, he says, was "institutional and bureaucratized misanthropy" which led to a deep complicity in the most terrible event of the last century, the Shoah. This leads him to call, in the closing chapters of the book, for a revised Christology, a re-envisaging of the cross, its de-emphasis as a Christian symbol, a new reformation, and a commitment by the Church to values of religious pluralism and democracy which he feels need reinforcement.

At the heart of this revised Christology—on which I will not comment because I do not feel qualified to comment on those aspects—James Carroll sees the question of the Jews. More specifically, he sees the hatred of the Jews, the record of denial and the negation of guilt that must be honestly dealt with. This is not, in Carroll's narrative, a marginal tragedy. It is, for him, the heart of the matter, and that is one of the things I find impressive in this book, the centrality which he is prepared to give to this issue.

James Carroll is not the first and he is not the last to explore antisemitism within the Catholic Church. However, there is something uncompromisingly authentic about his personal way of dealing with these issues and laying bare his own soul and the crisis in his own beliefs at various times in his life. He is not content with shallow explanations. He has no patience for those who would blame the Holocaust on something called neo-paganism or who would somehow seek to exculpate the Church as an institution from its responsibilities.

Carroll asks a central question about the role of the crucifixion in Christian piety and the fact that the Jews were perceived so early on in the New Testament itself and in the early centuries of Christian history as its enactors. Indeed, Carroll rejects the whole idea that God requires the suffering and death of Jesus as a source of salvation.

Throughout the book there is one of the most unequivocal rejections of supersessionism that one could expect to find of that replacement theology. Carroll argues that supersessionism, in the end, implies the elimination of the replaced. There is a categorical repudiation of the portrayal of Judaism as Christianity's negative other.

At times I have to wonder whether the wish is more powerful here than the reality. One must ask whether that history which is recounted here of Judaism as the quintessential negative other of Christianity really was avoidable. Carroll argues the case for an alternative history, for places where opportunities were not taken, choices were not made, and he gives some examples. But I, perhaps like many professional historians, remain skeptical about those alternatives, even while accepting that there is indeed choice in history. This particular history of Christianity's perception of Judaism is one where the dominant weight of the tradition, certainly until fairly recently, was so overwhelming that one has to wonder whether these alternative options were really as possible as he makes them appear.

One thing, which is powerfully stated in the first section of the book, is the context of Roman imperial power, a vision of the Roman war machine, of a totalitarian force against which the Jews waged a hundred year war. The Caesarism that is portrayed in this book is a reminder of the context in which Jesus was born, lived, acted, and was crucified. Here again, while this is not new, there is something graphic about the way in which the Romans remain in the Gospels as unindicted co-conspirators. Carroll reminds us also of the way in which the very beginnings of Christian anti-Judaism lie in a very complex situation of sectarian conflict among Jews themselves. This conflict was exacerbated by the Roman policy of divide and rule, and eventually by the spreading of the Gospels among the Gentiles. What we see here is Carroll's conviction that Jesus was and remained a Jew from beginning to end. The Christian messianic experience was originally a Jewish experience and was created out of Jewish hope. This aspect of Carroll's narrative is very well done.

Here I want to say something more personal that very much affected me in the reading of this book. It is the chapter, so topical now, that relates to the Temple and the Temple Mount. As I understand it, a key moment in Carroll's new understanding of Jesus and who he was, comes when he can envisage Jesus walking on the ramp leading to the Temple Mount. He is there not to throw out the moneychangers, as we learn from the familiar conventional reading of the New Testament. Instead, he is there to encounter God in the place that would reveal him, Jesus, as a Jew to his core, as part of Israel. He arrives at the site where God had touched the earth—in this place alone. This chapter shows us something unfamiliar, and yet so simple and blindingly obvious when it is stated, Jesus did not come to oppose or destroy the Temple. He came there because this was the navel of the world and the heart of Israel's faith.

I speak here coming from Jerusalem and Israel, on a subject that even for Israeli Jews themselves has suddenly returned with a stunning, unexpected, and visceral reality that transcends politics. Carroll describes with sorrow how the destruction of the Second Temple became, in the eyes of Christian theology, the validation that God had abandoned his people, the reprobate people who were doomed to wander in exile.

Yet God does not break his covenant. On this matter, I think James Carroll is in agreement with the present Pope, whatever their differences—and there are many— that subsequently appear in the book. I was very struck by a bold statement that Carroll makes in this context when he discusses the Pope's pilgrimage to Israel in April 2000. John Paul II is standing in devotion before the remnant of the Temple, and he is placing the written prayer in the crevice of the Western Wall asking for forgiveness for the sufferings through the centuries inflicted upon the Jewish people. This act, James Carroll writes, "was the single most momentous act of his papacy." This is a bold statement indeed, but I agree that this act was even more significant than the Pope's presence at Yad Vashem.

I will not dwell on the ways in which piece by piece, stone by stone, Carroll recounts the many "slanders" that were perpetrated against Judaism over the centuries. Some of these slanders are still operative and need to be challenged almost on a daily basis. There is, for example, the longstanding dichotomy between the God of the Old Testament and the New, the idea that the Old Testament God is a God of vengeance, a God of the law and revenge—"an eye for an eye, a tooth for a tooth"—and the New Testament God is a God of love, mercy, and forgiveness. I have heard this so many times, even from well-meaning, enlightened people who believe they are beyond all prejudice, but who unconsciously repeat this notion. It is important that it is observed and refuted in this book.

Let me pass to a critical issue that appears again and again through the book. What is the relationship between traditional, "normal" Christian anti-Judaism and modern, abnormal, racist, secular antisemitism? I think some important landmarks are laid out here. This is a difficult and controversial issue, and it cannot be casually dealt with by claiming there is an absolute separation between the two.

Carroll gives some indications of how and why this is not so. This is particularly true, with regard to what happened in the Iberian Peninsula in the 15th century and subsequently, especially with reference to the *limpieza de sangre*, the blood purity statute. He describes the special constellation of Spain, the situation of the *conversos*, who constituted one-third to one-half of the Jewish population of Spain. Within the Church itself, a notion of blood purity was legitimized, certainly within the Spanish Church.

The problem of how the papacy responded to racial antisemitism is more difficult. It was disapproved of and opposed, but not particularly strongly. The ravages of the blood purity notion, the sense of siege of the Church during the Counter-Reformation, and a messianic sense of the need for a rapid, swift conversion of the Jews led to a series of persecutory measures in the mid-16th century which had disastrous effects on the Roman Jews up to 1870.

Carroll dwells at great length on the Roman ghetto, sometimes overstating it. But I think there can be no questioning of the fact that the degradation of the Jews of Rome throughout nearly 300 years is a significant indicator of the very sickness that Carroll finds at the heart of a certain kind of Roman Catholicism: the cult of power, of doctrinal uniformity, and of intolerance.

Nevertheless I was puzzled at the fact that on four occasions, Carroll quotes Cardinal Cassidy as saying that the Roman ghetto—the Church-enforced ghettos—were "the antechamber of the death camps." I understand quoting it once or twice, but four times? Even if the Cardinal said it, is it necessarily true? As a Jew it might be convenient for me to hear this, but as a historian I am not necessarily convinced that this is the case. The Christian record is bad enough without having to invoke the gas chambers for enhanced effect.

Carroll dwells at great length and in an interesting way with the case of *La Croix* and France in the Third Republic when he analyzes the response of the Catholic Church to Jewish emancipation and to the challenge of liberalism and equality of rights. He describes the recently beatified Pius IX: his anti-liberalism and hostility to progress, his blind rejection of all the works of modernity, and the way in which this rigid stance almost inevitably impacted on the attitude and policy toward Jews. In the case of France, Carroll also gives some good, convincing illustrations of how the Catholic clergy were involved in antisemitic movements, congresses, and the politicization of antisemitism in the Third Republic.

I think that Carroll is right that Catholic involvement in antisemitic politics is one of the seedbeds of the subsequent catastrophe. Carroll could have reinforced the

French example with cases from other societies. Fin-de-siècle Austria was actually a far more effective example of the use of mass politics in the name of a populist Catholicism built largely on antisemitic appeals. This is indeed an important historical link because otherwise the preparatory phase that led up to the 1930s and 1940s does not make sense.

This leads me to my last point, which relates to Pius XII, to the 1930s, to the Church, and the Holocaust. I think there are some missing connections in the way that this period is presented in *Constantine's Sword*. This era is, of course, the subject for a book in its own right. Perhaps James Carroll needed a more rigorous editor who would have cut 100 pages from earlier sections, enabling him to deal with this period at greater length and with the depth that it requires. We need a more probing treatment of the acquiescence of the German Episcopate, for example: the ways in which leading cardinals such as Michael Faulhaber, Cardinal Bertram, and others accepted in silence, an escalation of anti-Jewish actions. They accepted the 1933 Boycott, the 1935 Nuremberg Race Laws, the 1938 *Kristallnacht* pogrom. They were silent at a time when a firm and sharp protest was still possible, well before the Final Solution. We know that the Catholic Church was capable of resisting Nazism, as its famous encyclical of 1937 demonstrated. Yet there was no word even then about antisemitism or specifically, about the German Jews as such. There were no explicit condemnations.

The explanation for this silence is not entirely clear in the book. Of course, it is not entirely clear for any of us. Not all the records have been opened. But I find that Carroll's explanation depends too much on an indictment of the papal will to power. This thesis has also been put forward by John Cornwell and it did not really convince me in that form either. Carroll and Cornwell both appear to argue that the heart of the problem concerning the behavior of the Catholic Church in the 20th century was its authoritarian tradition and nexus with imperial power. I agree that this was a contributing factor, but I do not see it as central to the issue of the Vatican's failure to respond effectively.

I, myself, have written extensively on the issue of antisemitism, and I cannot honestly say that I discovered anything new in the facts related in *Constantine's Sword*. The record is clear, yet there were moments where Carroll's unequivocal indictment of the Church seemed to me to be slightly overstated. That may seem surprising since I am not known as someone who has been particularly soft on the history of the Church regarding the Jews. Yet there are occasions when I might have wished for more nuance.

I am, however, full of admiration for the way that *Constantine's Sword*—whatever specific critiques one could address to it—unsparingly confronts all of us with the idea that Christian antisemitism is a question of the human condition itself. This is a rare example of a book where the tragedy of antisemitism is conveyed and communicated as a personal and existential question of conscience. I think that in this spirit we should accept it and rejoice that it has been written.

The Need for a Critique of the Institutional Church

Donald J. Dietrich

James Carroll's book reminds us that historians, theologians, and social scientists have an obligation to critique Christianity when it fails to live up to its normative origins. In a similar vein, Johannes Metz, a Catholic theologian, has insisted that theology itself has to cease being ahistorical. Metz has stated that if an event, the Holocaust for example, causes moral horror, then we have to question the historical theology and ideology behind it as well as the socio-historical dynamics that led up to the tragedy.

Historians usually respond to such a challenge by selecting data relevant to this issue of concern. But how can this data be packaged and presented? Academic and popular historians often make statements that need amplification through nuancing, and we never seem to have enough facts. For example, the links that James Carroll describes between the Second Reich, pan-German nationalism, and racism have been the subjects of countless books and articles that warn us against any kind of simplistic reductionism, when we deal with complex matters of history. Carroll's observations are basically correct, but we probably should see a bit more of the historical developments behind his assertions in order to fully grasp the reality of life in Bismarck's Germany, not to mention in European civilization as a whole. To have included even more details, however, would have made *Constantine's Sword* unwieldy.

As he packages the data, Carroll's historical analysis can be characterized as very personal, since his own life has become the lens through which he "reads" the facts. But such an approach is not bad. Along with Metz and others, Carroll has concluded that the Catholic Church itself has used an ahistorical theology to function in a world of contingent events and so has frequently hurt people. A personalized approach to history may help provide the remedy to some of the evils that have been perpetrated.

We may engage in the "yes, but" game of the professional historian and never get to the essence of the moral issues posed in this book. James Carroll has entered the realm of moral history, to borrow a phrase from author Jonathan Glover. In Glover's recent book, *Humanity: A Moral History of the 20th Century*, ethics interrogates history. The historian begins with an ethical stance and then looks back at the history of an institution in order to understand where that history went right and where it went wrong and why. In *Constantine's Sword*, Carroll looks back to assess the points at which the Catholic Church took wrong turns. His moral responses to antisemitism and the Shoah have helped him formulate the questions that make this a living book, sensitive to the historical tradition of Christianity.

In addition, Carroll's experiences have informed the questions that have guided his selection and organization of historical details in *Constantine's Sword*. He has selected what for him are the relevant details. Historians do this all the time. If historians are honest, we admit that any book we may write is only the beginning or the continuation of the conversation. Carroll and I would have to accept the fact that a really honest dialogue will never really end, since the historians as actors in the drama of the human condition change their minds or simply change. Then new concerns are brought to the table.

Carroll summarizes discussions of the last few decades and opens up new concerns. Even though the Catholic Church may not be racially antisemitic, it certainly was anti-Judaic in the political, economic, social, and religious arenas. As an institution it has been seriously corrupted through the ages. James Carroll has reminded us that institutions and systems can be sinful.

The "We Remember" document of March 19, 1998, reintroduced very forcefully the simmering controversy over whether the Church as such could sin. I was presenting a lecture at St. Mary's College in Minnesota when the document was published and was asked to give a response. I centered my comments on the notion, contained in the document, that the Church's sons and daughters may have participated in the Holocaust, but that the "Church as such" was not sinful. It was on this issue—that is the notion of the innocence of the Church as such—that I disagreed with the Vatican and not for the first time. It seemed to me that Vatican II was serious when its document stated that the Church was sinful because it is composed of sinners. In essence, the fathers of the Council were questioning the medieval and scholastic determination that the "Church as such" was an unblemished ideal and that the unfortunate evils of life only protruded through its members.

The social learning approach suggests that we humans form our culture and socialize our children through our institutions. Thus, we can have systemic and corporate evil, such as racism and antisemitism, within these institutions. Vatican II and various theologians since then have insisted that the Church is a "pilgrim" church and like all travelers, it can get lost and then has to find the correct way. Carroll shows us how the way was lost again and again.

The Church seriously lost its way when it decided to attack the modern project, liberalism, democracy, socialism, and freedom of conscience, by using a broad definition of antisemitism, not racism. Thus, Pius XI and Pius XII could attack Hitler's racist antisemitism while still nurturing the political, economic, and cultural antisemitism that would mandate removing Jews from positions prominent in society. Even Pius XI's "Hidden Encyclical" accepted this kind of antisemitism. Such an approach certainly softened the consciences of Europeans during the 1930s and made it difficult to respond to Hitler's menacing plans. I am sure that we are all amazed that these popes could think that restricting rights and human dignity at any level could occur without threatening life itself. Carroll is correct in saying that institutions which perform socializing functions have responsibilities and must bear some blame when evil occurs.

Since antisemitism was introduced so early in the Church's history, I would like to suggest a way to theologically re-enter the conversation between Christians and Jews. At the most fundamental level of theology, Christians need to emphasize God more than they have. They need to emphasize Jesus Christ the Savior more within the context of God's relationship to humanity. Christians too frequently center everything on Jesus, to the detriment of the God who sent him, guided him, and sustained him. Jesus subordinated himself to God's will in order to rule, co-serve, care for, and bring to fulfillment humanity and the universe in which humanity lives. The kingdom, that is, the rule of God, should rule theology. In essence, God rules over and loves and cares for Israel, the Church, and all nations.

For Christianity, the corollary of God's love (Father, Son and Spirit) for Israel is clear. What Jesus did and was and what Jesus Christ does and is in his Church today takes place within Israel. We see this in the life of Jesus, in the history of our two communities, and in the deeply Jewish roots of the Christian tradition which sustain us as Christians daily. The Israel on which the Church depends and within which it lives is not some abstraction found in a book, not a historically obsolete religion, nor a purely spiritual entity that somehow transcends this world. Israel is the actual living community of Jews with whom Christians live in a permanent relationship to this day.

Vatican III, which Carroll hopes will assemble, should include this dimension as it confronts the challenges of crafting a theology that is rooted in Christianity's normative origins. Only in this way will the Catholic Church be able to respond to the opportunities of embracing the pluralistic and human world that somehow is designed to bring God into a historical concreteness.

Apologia

Paul Mendes-Flohr

Guided by an eloquent pen and a probing, breathless honesty, James Carroll has taken us in *Constantine's Sword* "on a journey of moral reckoning through a history that culminates in the Shoah." This journey in Judaism is called a *heshbon nefesh.* It is soul-searching from the depths of one's soul, and the giving of an account of one's sins and misdeeds, both small and great, before God and one's fellow human beings. With unflinching candor, Carroll examines his soul and that of his Church with respect to the scandal of Jew-hatred, the theologically induced contempt of the People of Israel that culminated in the satanic nightmare we now call the Shoah.

In the language of his tradition, Carroll has written an *apologia*, a brief in defense of his client, the Catholic Church. However, unlike classic apologists who penned sophisticated but often tendentious arguments to fend off censure of the Church's doctrines and conduct, Carroll's defense of the Church (which he so manifestly loves) is to acknowledge its guilt and blame. His *apologia* is an extended apology. In acknowledging the cumulative wrongs committed by the Church and Christians against the Jews, he apologizes to the Jews. Like all genuine apologies, his words are animated by contrition and a desire to right the wrong, a reparation that cannot redress the horrors of the past or even heal the wounds of terrible memories. Rather, with an inconsolable gaze at the past, it is a reparation that is borne by a pledge to engage the Jewish people and their religious witness free of the theological prejudices that have erstwhile encumbered and poisoned Jewish-Christian encounter. Carroll presents his *heshbon nefesh* as an offering of hope. I would like to offer some reflections and celebration of the ethical and theological virtues of apology, as I share in his hope for an honorable and mutually respectful future between Christians, Jews, and all faith communities.

It seems to be a universal assumption that apology is an indispensable element of the grammar of interpersonal relations. We accidentally bump into someone, we apologize: *Entschuldigung, excusez-moi*, sorry, *slihah*. These are formulaic utterances usually recited reflexively without much thought or ceremony. Apologizing becomes more difficult and urgent when one has (or is perceived to have) offended or injured a significant other. Should one care, one must pause and consider the complaint of the other and take his or her point of view, feelings, and perception of a given event into account. Here apology is not reflexive, but reflective. It entails self-reflection and self-judgement.

If one cares about the other and one's relationship with the other, one is bound to allow the other to mirror one's behavior. To secure the dignity of our relationships with others, the image that others have of us and our views, our conduct must be refracted through the perceptions we have of ourselves. These competing images must often be negotiated. The other with whose plaint we must reckon may have misunderstood our intent, but the health of interpersonal relations requires that we at least acknowledge the other's annoyance and pain.

The German Jewish poet Heinrich Heine noted our responsibility for the anguish we may cause others, even inadvertently, in a brief poem.

Und hütte deine Zunge wohl,
Bald ist ein hartes Wort entflohen.
Oh, Gott, es war nicht Böse gemeint.
Der anderer, aber geht und weint.

And guard thy tongue,
Lest a harsh word escape.
Oh God, it was not meant in malice:
The other, goes and weeps.

Heine's insight is not particularly profound. One might even say it is banal—but who would deny that an awareness of how we affect others is essential for wholesome interpersonal relations?

Just as a self-reflective apologetic posture is an imperative for maintaining the fabric of everyday relations between individuals, it is no less of an imperative for inter-communal relations. The modern world has witnessed the ever-increasing emergence of communities from their isolation and self-enclosure. Communities no longer merely interact as in times of yore on an instrumental, commercial, economic, or political plane. They have come to share a cultural and, therefore, a social space of common ideas, values, and educational ideals. They now live not as before merely next to one another, but *with* one another.

This admittedly sweeping generalization is illustrated by the passage of Jewry into European civilization. Emerging in the 18th and 19th centuries from the ghetto—as my colleague Zwi Werblowsky once pithily remarked, with a bang and prolonged whimpers—the Jews quickly internalized the cultural ethos of their respective host societies. The space beyond the ghetto walls was not simply a new political and economic terrain, but also a new cognitive and axiological territory that Jews so adeptly learned to occupy. The change in cultural geography of Jewish life also obliged Jews to see themselves through the eyes of others. To be sure, the mirrors that the hosts held before them were often distorted and distorting. To the degree that Jews became acculturated and lost a firm rootedness in their own primordial culture, these mirrors became the only mirrors through which they beheld themselves. Bereft of an alternative, positive set of mirrors, the mirrors held up by their censorious neighbors frequently led them to a distorted self-image and left deep scars of shame and self-denigration. It was as if the Jews were placed in a house of distorting mirrors in which one only saw transmogrified images of oneself.

Within this context, apologetics have gained a bad reputation among Jews. Apologetics are seen as a dishonorable yielding to Gentiles' biased images of Jews and Judaism. Apologetics are, hence, regarded as a self-abnegating gesture towards total assimilation.

Yet, apologetics need not only be an act of fawning primed by a desperate desire to be accepted or free of those negative self-images that haunted the Jews as they left the culturally self-enclosed world of the ghetto. Deracination was not the fate of all Jews who sought to pitch their tents in the cultural and social terrain beyond the ghetto walls. While maintaining a firm grounding in Judaism and thus a healthy self-image, some Jews devised various strategies to live with multiple cultural and social identities. Concomitantly, Jews have learned to scrutinize themselves and their religious heritage through new critical lenses: by seeing themselves through the eyes of others with whom they lived and with whom they

73

wished to dwell in mutual respect and dignity. Living with others obliges one to take into account how others view your actions and attitudes. To ignore this challenge would be disingenuous. We must accept the possibility that our opinions and conduct as Jews might be hurtful to others. Just as in interpersonal relations, apology need not compromise the integrity of one's position, especially if the other's complaint is based on misperception. Apology is, nonetheless, dictated by the desire to honor the other's perceptions and feelings with whom one shares a cultural and social space.

In the past, Jewish-Christian relations were marked by an asymmetrical conflict. The Church was affiliated with the institutions of power and the Jews were perforce the victims of that power. The *heshbon nefesh*, the need to apologize, was and is hence preeminently a Christian obligation. The sheer magnitude of Christian civilization's sins—crimes—against the Jewish people renders any suggestion that Jews also owe Christians an apology utterly obscene.

Contemporary Jews, who by virtue of the rights bequeathed them by the democracies in which they live and *a fortiori* through the establishment of the State of Israel, are no longer bereft of power. Jews are no longer the victims of others' abuse of power; Jews no longer need to view interactions with others through the prism of victimhood. The dignity of empowerment bears the strength and responsibility to acknowledge one's own failings, and to view oneself with the eyes of the other. Scrutinizing oneself from the perspective of the other may also have a redemptive effect. As Franz Kafka noted in his diary after attending a Zionist meeting, the acknowledgement of "national faults can be very painful, but also very liberating."

Kafka was apparently referring to an address delivered by Martin Buber in Prague. Years later, writing from Jerusalem, Buber, the philosopher of dialogue, would observe that the Jewish question, which preoccupied Europe for centuries, was in fact, a Christian question. The treatment of the Jews was a recurring test of the efficacy of Christian values, doctrines, and ethical commitments. The restoration of Jewish political sovereignty, Buber continued, had not only radically transformed the political status of Jewry. It also confronted Judaism and its ethical and spiritual teachings with a test that years of exile and powerlessness had spared it. More pointedly, he held, just as the Jewish question was in effect a Christian question, the Arab question—as Zionists are wont to call the seemingly intractable conflict with the Arabs of Palestine—is ultimately a Jewish question.

One is reminded of the reaction of Max Brod, Kafka's friend and literary executor, who upon learning shortly after the First World War that there was an Arab population in Palestine which also laid claim to the land that Jewry regarded as its patrimony, jumped with joy, exalting, "Wonderful, we Jews, the children of prophets, will now be able to show the world how to resolve national conflicts." The tragic irony of Brod's naïveté only underscores the enormity of the challenge posed to Judaism by Jewry's assumption of political power.

Without elaborating, I conclude by restating my thesis. Following James Carroll's emotionally and spiritually courageous example, contemporary Jewry should affirm apology as an act of acknowledging with a contrite heart the hurt and harm that our attitudes and actions may cause others. The need to apologize from time to time is an ethic that must not only inform our interpersonal relations, but also our relations with other faiths and communities. Just as the liturgically prescribed *heshbon nefesh* on the Day of Atonement allows for reparation of our sins and the promise of spiritual renewal, the apologetic acknowledgement of others bears the promise of ensuring that the cultural and social space that we, the denizens of the modern world, share with our fellow human beings will sponsor our mutual spiritual and moral growth.

A Christian, Muslim, Jewish Encounter

Kanan Makiya

James Carroll's book brings to mind an encounter
between a Christian, a Muslim, and a Jew, an actual
historical event that took place a very long time ago. The
Christian was an old man by the name of Sophronius.
He was the patriarch of his city, Jerusalem, and he was
about to do the hardest thing he had ever been called
upon to do in his life: sign a treaty surrendering the
seat of his patriarchate and the crown jewel of his
entire belief system. And surrender it to whom? To an
upstart conqueror, a desert chieftain, and a barbarian, at
least this is how Sophronius must have viewed Umar
ibn al-Khattab, the second Caliph of Islam, and a close
companion of the Prophet Muhammad.

It is unlikely that Sophronius knew much of anything
about Umar or his religion, Islam. For one, the Quran had
not yet been put together into a single book, not at any
rate at the time of this meeting which historians think
must have taken place some time between 636 and 638
C.E.

To make matters worse for Sophronius, the third member
of the party was a Jew. He was Ka'b al-Ahbar, a very
learned man, perhaps even a rabbi, and he was Umar's

counselor and advisor on the holy sites of Jerusalem. I have called Ka'b a Jew, but in fact he had recently converted to Islam, probably in the year or two preceding this historic meeting. Ka'b is credited in the Muslim tradition as being the oldest source of Jewish ideas and traditions in Islam. His role as counselor, the reason for his presence at the meeting, and the enormous esteem he clearly commanded among the first generations of Muslims all derived from his Jewish learning. This is one justification for calling him a Jew in spite of his conversion.

What about Ka'b's new faith, acquired when he was in his late seventies or early eighties? What does it mean for a very old man—born and brought up as a Jew in Yemen, taught the Torah until he perhaps even became a teacher of it himself —to cut his roots, emigrate to Medina, and declare himself a follower of a far-away desert Prophet?

We do not really know what kind of a Muslim Ka'b was. But we know that there had long been deep affinities between the beliefs of the Arabs and the Jews, affinities one would never imagine existed if one were to judge by the way that Arabs and Jews frequently think about one another today. We know, for instance, that in Muhammad's time Jews used to read the Torah in Hebrew and interpret it to the Prophet's followers in Arabic. We know that allegiance to Muhammad as God's Messenger was all that conversion to Muhammad's religion entailed during those years in which Ka'b became some kind of a Muslim. You could be a Muslim and continue praying towards Jerusalem, as all Muslims used to do in the first years of Muhammad's mission. And Muhammad's followers fasted on the Jewish Day of Atonement in the first decade or two of his prophecy. In fact, one could be a Muslim and a Jew at the same time as long as one accepted the idea that the revelation that had descended upon Muhammad had come from God.

So the question arises: what was Ka'b? Was he a believer in Allah with all the meanings that later generations of Muslims read into that statement? Or was he a dissembling Jew, a fraud and an opportunist, as has been claimed by some Western scholars and modern Islamists alike?

The larger point that I am trying to make is that being a Muslim or a Jew at the time that Jerusalem became a Muslim city, 1,400 years ago, was worlds apart from being Muslim or Jewish today—just as being a Christian before Constantine was worlds apart from being Christian after the Emperor's ascent to power. The sibling rivalry between Christianity and Judaism took two centuries to form into completely distinct and antagonistic religious identities, as James Carroll has shown. The sibling relations between Judaism and Islam were still very much in flux at the time of our seventh century encounter. And it was not really a rivalry at all. In seventh century Jerusalem, the "sword" dividing Judaism and Islam had not yet fallen. It was a world in which all the roles were reversed from what we would expect given the abysmal state of Arab-Israeli relations and Muslim-Jewish relations today.

What was the meeting between Sophronius and Umar about? A transfer of sovereignty was taking place. A thoroughly Christianized Jerusalem—Constantine and his mother, the Empress Helena, had seen to that—was about to pass into the hands of a new Abrahamic faith, one that in those days ardently sought Jewish lore and scriptural interpretations. At the time of the meeting, Palestinian Jewry was in full decline, having experienced forced conversions and massive persecution in the previous two centuries. These events culminated in massacres, or pogroms, of Christians by Jews and of Jews by Christians during the interlude of Persian rule (615-630 C.E.). Persian rule was ended by the Emperor Heraklius on the very threshold of his own defeat by Umar's bedouin armies of believers. So a man like Sophronius, meeting his conqueror Umar ibn al-Khattab, one of the Prophet's closest companions and the second Caliph of Islam, was pickled in the juices of hatred of Jews preached in the sermons of John Chrysostom. Saint Augustine's moderating influence, which James Carroll writes about, was felt more in the West than it was in the East. For reasons that are made clear in *Constantine's Sword*, Sophronius would not have taken kindly to the presence of Ka'b al-Ahbar at the moment of his greatest humiliation and capitulation.

Why, one might legitimately ask, was Sophronius even present at the meeting? After all, the Byzantine army had been routed on the banks of the Yarmuk River a year or two earlier. The garrison of defenders left in Jerusalem had long since fled. Sophronius's cowardly commander was ensconced in Alexandria. Jerusalem was an island in a sea of enemies, the last city in the Fertile Crescent to fall to the Muslim armies. So what on earth was Sophronius doing there, dressed, as the sources tell us, in long silken robes with golden chains trailing after him?

He was there because the places of Jesus's life, suffering, death, burial, and resurrection were more important to him than life itself. We know that much about Sophronius from his writings. And we can understand the profound depths of emotion involved from reading James Carroll's book. At the heart of the Christian story, to paraphrase one of James Carroll's chapter titles, there was a place and that place was Jerusalem. On the strength of his feelings for that place, Sophronius had the gall to write to the Caliph Umar and offer him a peaceful transfer of sovereignty in Jerusalem, but on condition that he come in person all the way from Medina to receive the keys of the city. He did this knowing that the battle had already been lost from the military point of view. Still, he hoped to use the force of his personality and all the pomp and circumstance of Byzantine art, architecture, and ritual to wrest from his adversary some measure of protection for those places and churches and properties that meant so much to him as a Christian. To an extent, the strategy worked. The Caliph Umar (who incidentally has been compared to Saint Paul as a character and in the role he played in spreading Islam outside the confines of Arabia) was of course not won over to Christianity. But he did end up granting the wily Sophronius almost everything for which he asked, with one very important exception: a continuation of the ban on the presence of Jews in Jerusalem, a ban that dated back to the second century and the Emperor Hadrian. Jewish settlement in Jerusalem began to flourish under Muslim rule, after an interruption of nearly five centuries.

Muslim and Christian sources, both of which tell of this historic encounter between Sophronius and Umar, agree on two points. The first is that following the settlement of the terms of the city's capitulation, Sophronius took Umar—I would guess in the company of Ka'b, but the sources do not tell us that—on a tour of the Holy City. Both sets of sources also agree that Umar, who visited many fine churches, including the Church of the

Holy Sepulchre, really was interested in only one site. That site was the Temple Mount, known in the oldest Muslim sources as *mihrab Dawood*, the prayer place of the Prophet David. Along with Solomon, David features very prominently in the Quran.

At the time of the Muslim conquest, the Temple Mount was quite literally the city dump. The city that Empress Helena had forged into existence in the fourth century daily emptied its bowels onto the holiest site of Judaism. Whether this was deliberate or not is a matter of some debate among historians. But there is no disputing the fact that all Muslim historians in the classical period believed that it was deliberate. It was to this city dump that Umar insisted on going, in spite of Sophronius's attempts to dissuade him.

The story of what happened on the Temple Mount on that extraordinary occasion is the stuff of Muslim myth and legend. What is important is that the first Muslim city planning act—if I might call it that—in the Holy City which the Muslims now ruled and towards which they prayed. It provided for the cleaning of the Temple Mount and the exposure of the Rock that today lies graced by a building, the Dome of the Rock, perhaps the most famous symbol of Jerusalem for Palestinians and Israelis alike.

Why was the Dome of the Rock built, this first and oldest Muslim monument, this first great work of art and architecture of Muslim civilization, a building that looks today almost exactly what it looked like in the seventh century? The evidence suggests it was built to celebrate and revere a Jewish rock, the last remaining vestige of the long-gone Temple of the Jews, a relic that Jewish sages since the second century had vested with such importance that they called it *Even Shetiyah*, the Rock of Foundation, the navel of the universe, the site of Abraham's sacrifice and many other things. There is good reason to think that many or some of these associations were on Muslim minds when the Dome of the Rock was built. But it is also true to say we don't know exactly which of the many Jewish associations of the Rock appealed to the Muslims of that time.

Whatever those Jewish associations were in the seventh century—and scholars have debated the likelihood of this one versus that—there is no doubt whatsoever that none of those associations are on Muslim minds today. Both Muslims and Jews have forgotten, or deliberately erased from their historical traditions, all memory of their beginnings. You will not find Ka'b mentioned in a Jewish source. He was, after all, a renegade from the faith.

On the Muslim side the act of historical erasure of the facts was even worse. In 1946, an article was published entitled, "Ka'b al-Ahbar, the First Zionist." The author, a disciple of the Islamo-Arabist leader Rashid Rida, set out to prove that Ka'b, the oldest authority among Muslims on Jewish scripture, had been involved in a conspiracy to murder the Caliph Umar. The article was criticized by Muslim scholars and is by no means representative. But it is suggestive of the wounded and defensive mindset which has surfaced, I believe, on both sides since the creation of the State of Israel and the escalation of the Arab-Israeli conflict. A historical character like Ka'b al-Ahbar passes largely unappreciated by Muslims today, in part out of a fear that acknowledging his contribution might undermine the authenticity of Islam or the Muslim claim to Jerusalem. This kind of mindset led a senior Palestinian negotiator to ask his Israeli counterpart in the summer of 2000: "How do you know that your Holy Temple was located there [on the Haram]?" Not only are such fears belied by the whole pre-modern corpus of Muslim tradition, they make total nonsense of it.

In Muslim-Jewish relations it seems to me that we are looking at a tragedy still in the making, not one that is over. The dispute that erupted over the cross at Auschwitz was tempered by decades of hard work. *Constantine's*

Sword bears witness that the work of repairing Catholic and Jewish relations is perhaps not finished, but the book is in itself testimony that the work is well underway.

Sadly, such optimism is not imaginable in the case of Muslim and Jewish or Arab and Israeli relations today. The necessary repair work has not even begun. I hear nothing but accusations, ignorance, and intolerance flying over both sides of the barricades. Meanwhile another lightning rod for complete and total disaster is still standing in Jerusalem like the cross outside Auschwitz. I am referring, of course, to the Dome of the Rock.

Converts and the Jewish-Catholic Dialogue

Eva Fleischner

Our panel has been asked to look ahead. It has been difficult for me to turn away from the past toward the future. The past has never weighed quite as heavily on me as it did while I was reading James Carroll's long reflection. Over the past 30 years of dealing with the Shoah, with Christian antisemitism, and with the renewal of Vatican II, I have managed to remain basically hopeful. I have argued more than once with some of my students that the glass is half-full rather than half-empty. My hope has been severely tested in reading *Constantine's Sword*. When, at the end, I sat quietly for a time and looked at a small crucifix that I love, tears came to my eyes. And yet, James Carroll retains hope after years of living with and confronting the sins of our Church. Hope, then, is possible for us, also. Let me suggest three areas where I find signs of hope for the future.

I will take the chapter on Edith Stein as the starting point for my first and very delicate theme, that of Jews who convert to Christianity. At the beginning of Christianity, the followers of Jesus saw themselves and were seen as good Jews. But at least since the early Middle Ages, the fate of Jewish converts to Christianity has been tragic.

Cut off from and by their fellow Jews, they often did not find a real home in their new Christian community. And, this is part of their tragedy: they often had internalized the negative Christian stereotypes of Jews. We know that even the great Edith Stein is reported to have spoken of the guilt of her "unbelieving people," even though she was ready to share their fate. Jewish converts to Christianity were, and still often are, considered traitors to their people. Indeed, in some cases they were: Torquemada, I suppose, is the most flagrant example. I do not find the impulse to convert surprising, given the extensive restrictions, pogroms, and expulsions which Jews suffered at the hands of Christians. No wonder some wanted out and even tried to curry favor with the enemy.

Must this situation continue? Let me suggest two reasons why I think it need not. First, if the Church succeeds in truly purging itself of supersessionism and religious absolutism, a process begun by Vatican II but still far from complete; and if consequently it develops a relationship of genuine equality and respect for Judaism, the day may come when Jews will no longer feel hostile toward those who convert to Christianity. There will always be conversions on both sides, since the spirit breathes where she will. The Church's efforts since *Nostra Aetate* and last year's epoch-making *Dabru Emet* are signs that a genuine new relationship between our two communities is possible at last.

Second, in a recent conversation, Krister Stendahl observed that some of the leaders in the Jewish-Catholic dialogue who have made enormous contributions are converts from Judaism. I mention only two, whom I have known well personally: Gregory Baum and John Oesterreicher. The latter, after an initial phase in which he advocated the conversion of Jews, eventually won their trust and made a very important contribution to *Nostra Aetate*. I also want to mention here the Cardinal Archbishop of Paris, Jean-Marie Lustiger, who overcame, literally, mountains of mistrust, a mistrust felt not only among Jews, but also among some of us Catholics. Yet, ever since he was interviewed by two very sharp Israeli journalists, he is spoken of by many in Israel as "our brother, the Cardinal of Paris." Lustiger's mother died in Auschwitz and he refuses to deny or let go of his Jewish roots. When I interviewed him in Paris in 1985, he told me that he had more invitations to synagogues for Shabbat, week after week, than he could possibly keep up with.

This trend, if it is indeed a trend, of Jews who become Christian and who, subsequently, play a leading role in the Church's new understanding of Judaism may bring about a new relationship of the convert to his or her Jewish community. It may give birth to trust and acceptance in place of rejection and resentment.

I should, however, mention what may prove to be a new
obstacle to a more positive relationship, one that is still
a living memory and that goes back to the Shoah. I
refer to the Church's attitude toward baptized Jews during
those terrible years. Although, in many cases, baptized
Jews ultimately shared the fate of other Jews—whether in
ghettos or in deportations or in the camps—they occupied
a privileged place in the eyes of the Church. They were
considered children of the Church, and as such they were
the object of repeated protests and interventions on the
part of Church authorities, protests which were made all
too rarely, if at all, on behalf of other Jews. While this was
the direct result, I believe, of the teaching of contempt
rather than—at least in most cases—of the converts' own
efforts, it is not surprising that this privileged position
often aroused hostility against Jewish converts among
Jews, as evidenced in the literature of the Shoah. Thus,
while we may have some new possibilities today, we are
still, I believe, heavily burdened by the baggage of history.
Indeed, we may have acquired a new bag since the Shoah.

Let me go on to a second sign of hope for the future.
Much of the sharpest criticism of the Church and of its
anti-Judaism is today coming from the pens of women
and men who persist in calling themselves Catholic and
who refuse to be driven out of the Church. By dint of their
lay status and because most of them are not members
of Catholic theological faculties, these authors have a

freedom denied to some theologians today. Their books often receive negative reviews by fellow Catholics, some of whom accuse them of betraying the Church. But, given the level of theological sophistication among the Catholic laity today and the growing number of lay theologians, I believe they can neither be silenced nor marginalized, as happened in the Middle Ages to Peter Abelard and to Nicolaus of Cusa, and today to some distinguished theologians. We may hope that books such as *Constantine's Sword* will reach a wide readership in Europe and also in Rome, and create a groundswell which may eventually lead to the new Council advocated by James Carroll. It would not be the first time that major changes in Church teaching have come about as a result of movements that began at the lay and grassroots levels.

A brief aside here. The moral outrage and anguish so evident in James Carroll's book is, I believe, a very healthy form of self-criticism. If and when "the Church as such"—to use an increasingly controversial term— comes to engage in such self-criticism, without any qualifying clauses such as those we have in the 1998 statement "We Remember," it will have achieved something of that honesty and self-criticism which are such admirable characteristics of the Hebrew scriptures.

Finally, I can only mention here briefly the new field of creation spirituality. Arising out of the new cosmology, it is revolutionizing our view of the universe and of humanity's place in it, and can help shape the new agenda, particularly with regard to Christology. As our view of the Christian mystery and of Christ's presence in this vastly expanded and expanding cosmos evolves, it will affect, as any Christology must, the Church's view of itself, and of Jews and Judaism.

The Lessons of *Constantine's Sword* for Jewry and Judaism

Irving Greenberg

Constantine's Sword is remarkable for the sweeping nature of the narrative, its full-heartedness, its ability to let go of the fig leaves, and to take responsibility for past Catholic/Christian failures without resorting to the natural self-protective conservative evasions. This, of course, is possible because the book is written by an individual, James Carroll, a writer who is a loving critic of the Catholic Church from within.

The Church *has* begun to address many of the concerns that James Carroll raises. But people and institutions that have the historic responsibility for carrying a magisterium of the past into the future understandably try to soften, modify, and hold back. Were Carroll's stance the Church's official position, it would be transformative of Jewish–Catholic relations in ways that we cannot even imagine at this moment.

Constantine's Sword is not the product of the Church establishment. Therefore, it is not clear that its vision will ever be realized. But one should acknowledge that the book is prophetic. The word "prophetic" is a tribute and it is a tribute to Catholicism itself. Even if James Carroll's ideas fail to become Church policy, it is a tribute to Catholicism that this tradition is able to nurture people so loyal to God, so devoted to the vision of creation and perfection, that they are capable of challenging their own tradition on its deepest level. Jews should avoid repeating the error of past unfortunate Christian polemics in which the prophets' self-criticism of Jewry and Judaism was misused and presented as "proof" of the inadequacy of Judaism. Such self-criticism is in fact a sign of profound spiritual resources and moral health.

Jews would do well to imitate and apply to ourselves the high level of moral standards that James Carroll has set for his own faith. Because we Jews focus so intensely on the events of the Shoah, we have not often enough asked ourselves the same kinds of questions which Carroll has addressed to his own tradition. We seldom put our own religion through rigorous self-criticism and testing.

I am not suggesting a *quid pro quo*. I am not saying that because some Catholics criticize themselves, that Jews should undertake self-criticism as well. I am saying that we can learn from the greatness of the human heart. When we see a model of purity and of religious inspiration and of moral fervor, the appropriate application is to imitate it in our own faith and our own practice.

Christianity is a religion of extraordinary power which has brought redemptive faith in God and the sense of God's love to billions of people. In the modern world, it is one of the main forces challenging materialism and abuse of power. It played a role in Poland in overthrowing the dictatorship of communism. It continues to play a role in Asia, such as in challenging caste societies in India. These instances add up to a remarkable religious contribution. However evil Christian mistreatment of Judaism has been, one at least has to stop and recognize the spiritual wealth and moral strength it has given throughout the human world. Jews are often afraid to give Christianity this kind of affirmation, in part because of religious insecurity. We worry that if we admit Christianity's strengths, all the Jews will be swept up and converted. But if we agree with James Carroll that the negative stereotyping of Jews must end, then we Jews should do unto others what we would have others do unto us. If we gave up our own pejorative categorization of other faiths, then on the merits we would entertain a more positive view of Christianity, especially as it is purified and ennobled by Carroll's work.

James Carroll calls for an end to "the sword" in Catholicism, arguing that the act of enforcement corrupts religion. There is a Jewish counterpart. Orthodoxy as established in Israel should give up the political power that it has amassed for itself. It should stop seeking the political and financial favoritism that it obtains by exploiting democratic opportunities and institutions. As an Orthodox Jew, I speak on this subject with particular pain and authority. Orthodox willingness to give up enforceability would be an appropriate religious and moral counterpart to James Carroll's call to Catholicism to give up the power of coercion and to enforce even "good" religion.

Carroll also speaks of ending the racial definition of Judaism—which in his judgment has crept into Christianity. As a Jewish thinker, I believe that Carroll does not do full justice to the positive implications of Jews by genetic inheritance (i.e., Israel of the flesh) and of election by birth. Still, I would urge that Judaism, too, has a lot of work left to do in assuring that concepts like "chosenness" do not degenerate into tribalism or into some form of absolute weight for biology in its religious categories. That form of absolutism is, in fact, disrespectful of the elements of choice and human responsibility which are equally important in Jewish tradition.

We need to focus on how Jews think of Christians. We are living after 40 years of serious (albeit sometimes limited and ambivalent) self-revision and self-criticism among Christians, especially among Catholics. This is not your grandfather's Christianity. We Jews should not be afraid to admit how much Christian attitudes have changed and how much of this has been said publicly. References to past acts of Christian discrimination as if nothing has been revised should stop. This will take a certain resolve on the part of Jews who are aware of these changes to speak up and condemn anti-Christian statements by those who are not aware of the new approaches.

There is still a fundamental judgment among the traditional sector of Judaism that Christianity is idolatry. This judgment is sometimes blurred; sometimes it is hidden and evaded, but it is persistent. This attitude creates ugly possibilities of immoral behavior towards Gentiles and needs to be challenged from within.

It is painful to correct such views; it is painful even to talk about them. But the alternative is to let the cancer of prejudice and contempt grow. Because we are living in an age of Jewish power, contempt is a much more dangerous cancer. When Jews harbored anti-Christian sentiments in the past, it was more justified because Jews were indeed oppressed by Christians. Furthermore, Jews had no power to act on their anti-Christian feelings. Now, however, Jews have developed power. They have the capacity to inflict serious damage on others, so they need to examine the feelings toward others and the traditions that might lead to abuses of their power.

I find James Carroll's ideas about "the holiness of democracy" particularly powerful, because I believe that integrating this idea is a challenge that both Catholicism and Judaism face together. We are living in an age of unparalleled freedom. With that freedom comes not only incredible power to upgrade the dignity of human life, but also new levels of human responsibility. We have sources of power unmatched in human history. We need to take theological and spiritual responsibility for our use of that power.

For centuries, people have believed that the authority of the past prevented them from dealing with these internal problems. Or they hid behind the belief that the immovable authority of the past is of such weight that believers cannot quarrel with them. Therefore, the faithful are exempted from addressing these problems directly. We now understand that the contemporary community of faith has the responsibility and the capacity to challenge problematic texts. We can do so without the arrogance of the first stage of modernity, in which liberals too often sought to dispose of and dump classic texts as if they were simply the shards of "primitive traditions" that we had inherited.

In today's post-modern situation, we can understand the authority and the sanctity of ancient texts, but we also know that we cannot dodge the problematics and the ugliness that they sometimes carry with them. We have the responsibility to confront those texts lovingly, in all their authority, but with all the authority that we have of being responsible for the moral world which we create. Do Christians have the capacity as Christians to challenge the New Testament itself? Carroll shows that the answer is yes. Then one must ask: Do Jews have the capacity as Jews to confront the Bible and the Talmud when they see texts that are deeply problematic?

If we understand what God has called us to do in our time, we will realize that all this is our responsibility. If the ultimate divine dream was to be worshiped by free people, then the time has come to take responsibility for our part of the covenant. Our calling is not only to perfect the world politically, economically, and socially, but to perfect the world spiritually and to truly be the "co-creators" of the tradition from Sinai.

Jews should also welcome Carroll's call for a new Christology. Carroll argues for a shift away from the notion that God demands the sacrifice of Jesus' life in order to forgive sins of mankind towards a deeper sense of Jesus as a proleptic messiah. I have argued elsewhere that Jews should not see Jesus as a false messiah—which suggests wrong values, wrong teaching, wrong direction—but as a *failed* messiah, by which I mean to identify a person who achieved extraordinary goals but did not succeed in liberating the whole world. To be a failed messiah requires very great spiritual force. Reaching this level is an extraordinary achievement in itself. Very few people in history have gotten that far. On their part, Jews should see Jesus as an example of Judaism's power to generate redemption and redeemers. Even if those redeemers do not bring the final perfection, they should be honored, learned from, and seen as people who incorporated in their own lives divine breakthroughs toward achieving the will of God, toward the perfection, transformation, and the redemption of humanity.

That kind of Jewish affirmation opens the door not only to a new Christology, but to a much broader understanding of how religions relate to one another. Freedom and mutual respect ultimately require all faith traditions to give up what has historically been their single most powerful center of gravity: the sense of the "in-group," the sense of the "otherness" of outsiders.

100

The great calling of religions—Judaism, Christianity, and every other religion—is to be partners with God, to redeem the world. The particular challenge for Christians is to transform the cross from a symbol of sacrifice into a driving force for affirming the power of life. That power can only remain a source of life when religions are in partnership with one another.

I believe that we can imagine a future in which Judaism embraces pluralism with the same commitment and respect for diversity that Jews ask of Christians. We can imagine a partnership in which both religions affirm the image of God in every individual and advance the idea that every individual is of infinite value and entitled to be heard. That kind of understanding needs also to go beyond Judaism, Christianity, and Islam—the monotheistic religions—to include the recognition that Buddhism, Hinduism, and other religions make important contributions to the spiritual life of the world.

Let us create a partnership to develop models in which religions can envision a "multi-centered relationship" to God. *Each* people is chosen. Chosenness can still be appreciated as an experience of God's love and of God's singling out. But it need not be falsely universalized into a claim of exclusivity. God practices multiple choice.

Even if James Carroll's message goes unheeded, I remain optimistic that progress between Jews and Christians can continue at a slower pace. Judaism and Christianity—particularly Catholicism—can build on the past 40 years of work together to build ever greater understanding and mutual respect. If, on the other hand, we can speed up the process and adopt the impatience, the moral purity of Carroll's position, then I believe both religions together might even succeed in bringing the messiah. That, after all, is what both religions are all about.

Author Biographies

James Carroll is a novelist and a journalist whose writings on politics, religion, and culture have challenged thinkers and government leaders in the United States and all over the world. He has studied poetry and religion, and has worked as a civil rights activist and a professor. In 1969, he became Catholic chaplain at Boston University, but left the priesthood in 1974 to write full-time. Carroll has published nine novels, including *The City Below*, a *New York Times* Notable Book, and numerous award-winning works of nonfiction, such as *An American Requiem: God, My Father, and the War that Came Between Us*, which won the National Book Award in 1996. His weekly column in *The Boston Globe* reminds readers of the moral imperatives that govern all people in a pluralistic society. His latest book, *Constantine's Sword: The Church and the Jews: A History*, was released in January 2001.

Donald Dietrich is professor of church history in the Department of Theology at Boston College. Among other publications, he has written *Catholic Citizens in the Third Reich: Psycho-Social Principles and Moral Reasoning* and *God and Humanity in Auschwitz: Jewish-Christian Relations and Sanctioned Murder*. He is currently doing research and publishing on patterns of resistance, dissent, and non-conformity among Catholics in the Third Reich.

Eugene Fisher is director of Catholic-Jewish Relations for the Secretariat for Ecumenical and Interreligious Affairs of the National Conference of Catholic Bishops (NCCB), a position he has held since 1977. Prior to 1977, Fisher was director of Catechist Formation for the Archdiocese of Detroit, as well as adjunct professor of Sacred Scripture at St. John's Seminary and at the Religious Studies Department of the University of Detroit. He has published 20 books and monographs and over 250 articles in major religious journals.

Eva Fleischner, a Roman Catholic theologian, is professor *emerita* at Montclair State University. Fleischner is on the advisory boards of the U.S. Bishops Office of Catholic-Jewish Relations and the Catholic Institute for Holocaust Studies of Seton Hill College. She is also a member of the Vatican Historical Commission, reviewing archival material relating to the Vatican during World War II. Fleischner is the author of many publications, including *Cries in the Night: Women Who Challenged the Holocaust*, which she coauthored with Michael Phayer.

Arthur Green is Philip W. Lown Professor of Jewish Thought at Brandeis University. Green has previously taught at the University of Pennsylvania and the Reconstructionist Rabbinical College, where he served as dean and president. Green is the author of several books, including *Tormented Master: A Life of Rabbi Nahman of Bratslav; The Language of Truth: Teachings from the Sefat Emet of Rabbi Judah Leib Alter of Ger;* and *These Are the Words: A Vocabulary of Jewish Spiritual Life.*

Rabbi Irving Greenberg is president of the Jewish Life Network and chair of the U.S. Holocaust Memorial Council. He also served as founding president of CLAL— The National Jewish Center for Learning and Leadership, rabbi of the Riverdale Jewish Center, associate professor of history at Yeshiva University, and founder, chair, and professor in the Department of Jewish Studies of City College of the City University of New York. Rabbi Greenberg has published numerous articles and monographs on Jewish thought and religion, including *The Jewish Way: Living the Holidays* and *Living in the Image of God: Jewish Teaching to Perfect the World.*

Kanan Makiya is a professor in the Near Eastern and Judaic Studies department at Brandeis University. In October 1992, he acted as the convenor of the Human Rights Committee of the Iraqi National Congress. He has collaborated on two films for television, the most recent of which was shown in the United States under the title *Saddam's Killing Fields*, and received the Edward R. Murrow Award for Best Television Documentary on Foreign Affairs in 1992. He is the author of several publications including *Republic of Fear* and *Cruelty and Silence: War, Tyranny, Uprising and the Arab World.*

Paul Mendes-Flohr is professor of modern Jewish thought at the Divinity School at the University of Chicago. His major research interests include modern Jewish intellectual history; modern Jewish philosophy and religious thought; German intellectual history; and the history and sociology of intellectuals. Together with Peter Schäfer, Mendes-Flohr serves as the editor-in-chief of a 22-volume German edition of the collected works of Martin Buber. He has written *German Jews: A Dual Identity* and is currently completing a biography of Franz Rosenzweig.

Daniel Terris is director of the International Center for Ethics, Justice and Public Life at Brandeis University. He also oversees the Brandeis Seminars in Humanities and the Professions, which provide programs on professional values and ethics using literary texts as the basis of discussion for professionals around the United States. Terris has written on 20th-century art, politics, and religion.

Robert Wistrich is Dr. Erich and Foga Neuberger
Professor of Modern Jewish History at Hebrew University.
His research interests include the history of
antisemitism; modern Jewish history in the 19th and
20th centuries; anti-Zionism; and nationalism and racism
in contemporary Europe. Among many publications,
Wistrich is the author of *Who's Who in Nazi Germany;*
Theodor Herzl: Visionary of the Jewish State; and *Anti-
Zionism and Antisemitism in the Contemporary World.*

*Special thanks to Melissa Holmes Blanchard, staff writer
at the International Center for Ethics, Justice and Public
Life, for her assistance with the editing of this volume.*

Centers

The International Center for Ethics,
Justice and Public Life

The International Center for Ethics, Justice and Public
Life exists to illuminate the ethical dilemmas and
obligations inherent in global and professional leadership
with particular focus on the challenges of racial, ethnic,
and religious pluralism. Examining responses to past
conflicts, acts of intervention, and failures to intervene,
the Center seeks to enable just and appropriate responses
in the future. Engaging leaders and future leaders of
government, business, and civil society, the Center
crosses boundaries of geography and discipline to link
scholarship and practice through programs, projects, and
publications.

The Bernard G. and Rhoda G. Sarnat Center for
the Study of Anti-Jewishness

The mission of the Bernard G. and Rhoda G. Sarnat
Center is to promote a deeper understanding of the
genesis, causes, nature, and consequences of anti-Jewish

prejudice, and Jewish and non-Jewish responses to this phenomenon, especially in North and South America, from both a historical and contemporary perspective. The Center supports research, lectures, and conferences, and carries out activities in partnership with other universities and organizations.

Contact Information

The International Center for Ethics, Justice and Public Life
Brandeis University
Mailstop 086
Waltham, MA 02454-9110
781-736-8577
781-736-8561 FAX
ethics@brandeis.edu
www.brandeis.edu/ethics

The Bernard G. and Rhoda G. Sarnat Center for the Study of Anti-Jewishness
Brandeis University
Mailstop 075
Waltham, MA 02454-9110
781-736-2125
tauber@brandeis.edu